THE LONG GALLERY DESIGN LIBRARY — TLG

thelonggallery.blogspot.com
twitter: @thelonggallery

Online News & Community for Medieval, Tudor & 19th-20th Century Revival Architecture, Style, Art & Design. The Long Gallery Design Library was established to preserve and disseminate valuable written and illustrated works relating to art, design, architecture and relevant historical topics covered by our website.

---

american biblioverken

Publishers of Quality Books

www.biblioverken.co.nr
twitter: @biblioverken

Also specializing in custom book, catalog, magazine and newsletter publishing for the architectural, heritage, real estate and arts sectors.

SCHWEITZER

schweitzercomm.blogspot.com
twitter: @schweitzercomm

Specializing in advertising, marketing, public relations and promotional materials and communications plans for the architectural, heritage, real estate, non-profit, education and arts sectors.

WILLIAM MORRIS

Some Thoughts Upon His Life : Work & Influence

Originally published by
THE CRAFTSMAN MAGAZINE
United Crafts, Eastwood, NY.
Irene Sargent - Author
- 1901 -

New Edition, Published 2018 by
AMERICAN BIBLIOVERKEN
Akron, Ohio USA

II

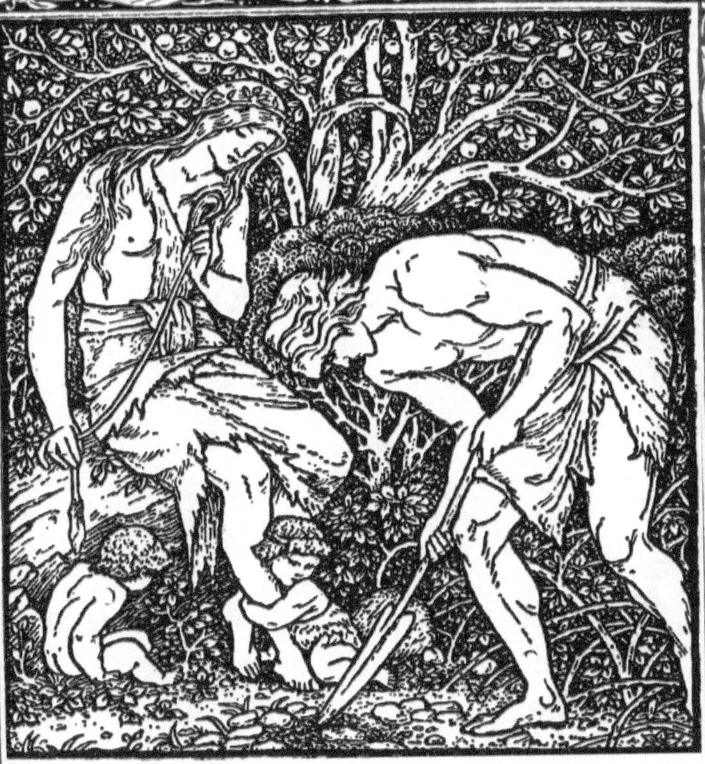

WILLIAM MORRIS
Some Thoughts on His Life : Work & Influence

The Craftsman Magazine

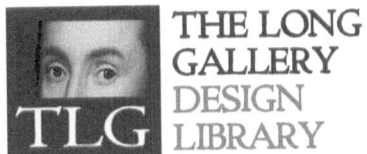

THE LONG GALLERY DESIGN LIBRARY

WILLIAM MORRIS
Some Thoughts on His Life : Work & Influence

Originally published 1901 as a feature in
THE CRAFTSMAN MAGAZINE

NEW EDITION - Design & Layout - Copyright 2018
american biblioverken

859 Bridge Road - Akron, Ohio 44312 - USA

ISBN - 1983825603

ISBN-13 - 978-1983825606

american biblioverken
PUBLISHERS

www.biblioverken.com

CONTENTS

Publisher's Notes   V

Foreward   1

William Morris: Some thoughts upon his life, art and influence   7

William Morris: His career as a Socialist   23

The firm of Morris & Company, Decorators   33

The Opera of "Patience" and the Aesthetic Movement   43

Two Friends: Morris & Burne-Jones   49

From The Craftsman:

An argument for simplicity in Household Furnishings   57

Style and its Requisites   63

IV

PUBLISHER'S NOTES

For lovers of Art & Design, particularly the work created during the late 19th and early 20th centuries, William Morris is an icon who not only produced great works of art and literature himself, but who also influenced how a generation of artists approached their work and the way it was created. In this, the third volume in our modest Design Library, we are presenting another classic work—this time not by Morris himself, but an analysis of Morris and his influence by a later American contemporary.

This original extended essay appeared in *The Craftsman*, a popular American magazine that was published by United Crafts, the well-known design, craft and furniture firm established by Gustav Stickley, who was himself a famous American design leader, furniture manufacturer and publisher. Stickley is recognized as a leading figure of the American Arts & Crafts Movement, and was a fearless proponent of its focus on simplified design, quality materials, and hand-made craftsmanship.

In addition to the Foreward and the main essay, the end of the book also includes some brief articles and notes about Stickley's own craftsman furniture and his studio's overall approach. Most of the illustrations feature images of his firm's furniture, as well as some contemporary examples of rooms where it was used.

FOREWORD

WITH the initial number of "The Craftsman," The United Crafts of Eastwood, N. Y. enter upon a work for which they hope to gain the sympathy and the co-operation of a wide public. The new association is a guild of cabinet makers, metal and leather workers, which has been recently formed for the production of household furnishings. The Guild has had but one parallel in modern times, and this is found in the firm organized in London, in 1860, by the great decorator and socialist, William Morris, together with his not less distinguished friends, Burne-Jones, Rossetti and Ford Madox Brown, all of Pre-Raphaelite fame.

The United Crafts endeavor to promote and to extend the principles established by Morris, in both the artistic and the socialistic sense. In the interests of art, they seek to substitute the luxury of taste for the luxury of costliness; to teach that beauty does not imply elaboration or ornament; to employ only those forms and materials which make for simplicity, individuality and dignity of effect.

In the interests of the workman, they accept without qualification the proposition formulated by the artist-socialist:

"It is right and necessary that all men should have work to do which shall be worth doing, and be pleasant to do; and which should be done tinder such conditions as would make it neither over-wearisome, nor over-anxious."

FOREWORD

The great results accomplished by the Morris firm grew out of the decoration of a single house: the first family dwelling of the Master himself. Then, the work extended with its deep, restorative influence, transforming the outward and decorative side of life, adorning the English home with the pleasures of art; until, in the opinion of a well-known critic, it had "changed the look of half the houses in London and substituted beauty for ugliness all over the kingdom." With this example before them, The United Crafts will labor to produce in their workshops only those articles which shall justify their own creation; which shall serve some actual and important end in the household, either by adding to the ease and convenience of life; or yet by furthering the equally important object of providing agreeable, restful and invigorating effects of form and color, upon which the eye shall habitually fall, as the problems of daily existence present themselves for solution. Thus, it is hoped to co-operate with those many and earnest minds who are seeking to create a national, or rather a universal art, adjusted to the needs of the century: that is, an art developed by the people, for the people, as a reciprocal joy for the artist and the layman.

Another object which The United Crafts regard as desirable and possible of attainment is the union in one person of the designer and the workman. This principle, which was personally put in practice by Morris, extended throughout his workshops; the Master executing with his own hands what his brain had conceived, and the apprentice following the example set before him as far as his powers permitted. The divorce between theory and practice was everywhere strenuously opposed, with the direct aim of creating and perfecting the art-artisan. In accepting the Morris principle, the United Crafts recognize all that it implies: First: the raising of the general intelligence of the workman, by the increase of his

FOREWORD

leisure and the multiplication of his means of culture and pleasure. Second: a knowledge of drawing as a basis of all the manual arts and as one of the essentials of a primary education which shall be worthy of the name.

With this general intelligence as working capital, the United Crafts do not exact from their members an innate manual dexterity, but. strictly in accordance with the Morris principle, they employ the nearest available aid to accomplish the work at hand. In this way, interest and a pleasurable excitement are awakened in the workman, and the thing created by his brain and hands becomes the child of his love which he seeks to develop and beautify to the extent of his own resources.

Again, as the tendency toward co-operation and constructive Socialism is one of the most marked signs of the times, the United Crafts purpose to extend their influence by forming groups of associates at numerous favorable points throughout the country; these associates being at will active workers and handicraftsmen; or yet again, business firms or private individuals who desire to build up a national art based upon sound aesthetic and economic principles. As the simplest means at their disposal of making known their existence and objects, the United Crafts have founded the monthly periodical of which the present number is the first issue. The position now taken by the publication will be maintained, and each successive number will deal with the relations of art to labor.

As is most fitting, the initial monograph is a criticism and study upon the life and work of William Morris, whose talents, time, energies and fortune were devoted to practical attempts toward peaceful revolution and reformation in popular art and in the condition of the workman. The article, based upon the two recognized authorities, Mackail and Aylmer Vallance, is a simple

FOREWORD

statement of fact, accompanied by inferences and deductions which are natural and obvious.

The second number of "The Craftsman" will follow with a similar monograph upon John Ruskin, whose influence was an important factor in the artistic and ethical development of William Morris, as is evidenced by the letters written during the tatter's student days at Oxford. The phase of Ruskin to be considered, is his attitude toward the great building-art of the Middle Ages, which grew out of an intense civic and co-operative spirit, whose pulsations were felt until the negations of the Renascence period forever stilled and nullified them. The new subject will be another plea for an art developed by the people, for the people, and in which the craftsman and the citizen shall be intimately allied.

In a subsequent issue, the "Rise of the Guild System in Europe" will be considered, with a maintenance of the same point of view, from which art will be regarded not as something apart from common and every-day existence, but rather as the very means of realizing life.

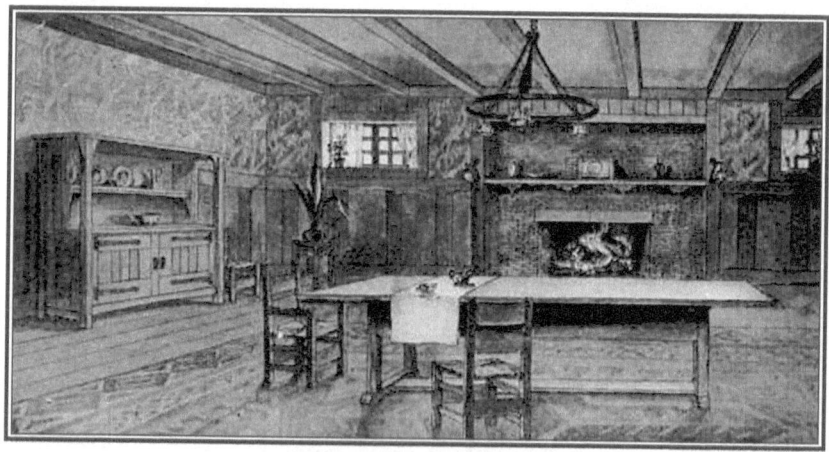

Suggestions for a Dining Room.

FOREWARD

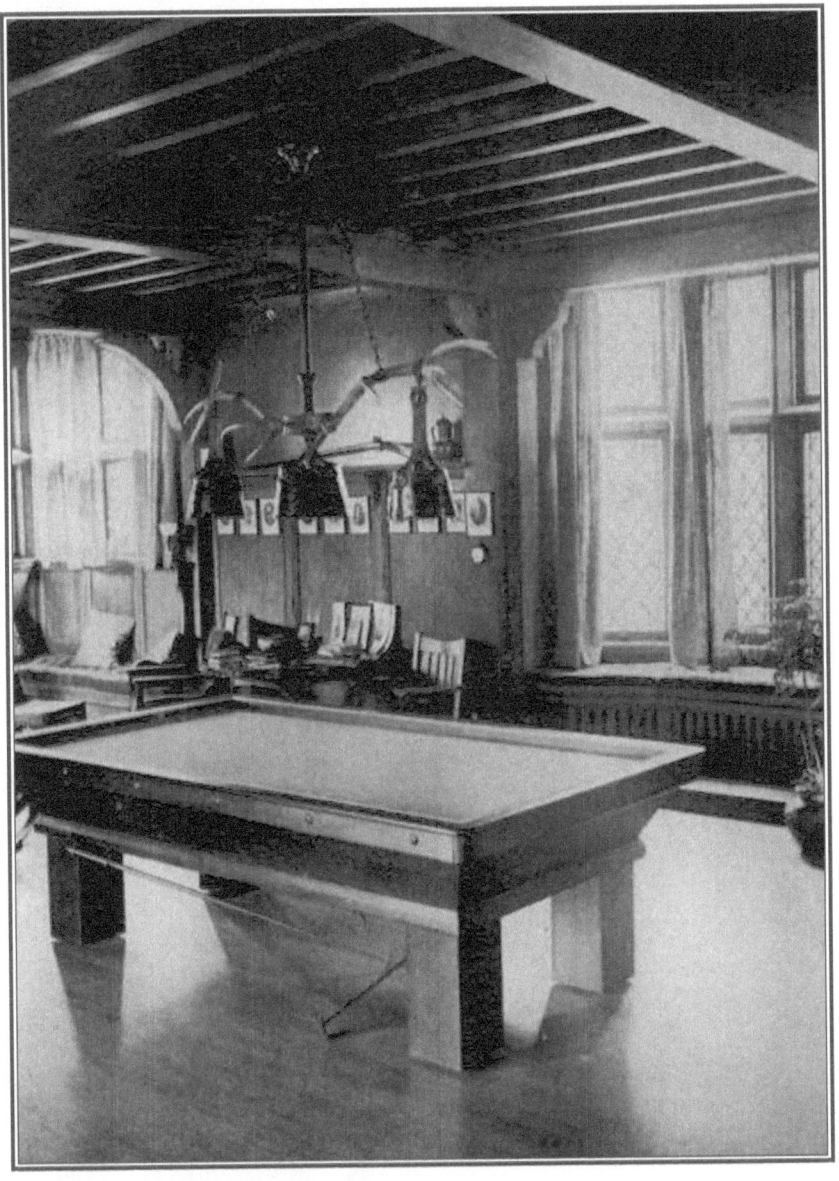

Billiard Room of Ernest J. White, Syracuse, NY

FOREWORD

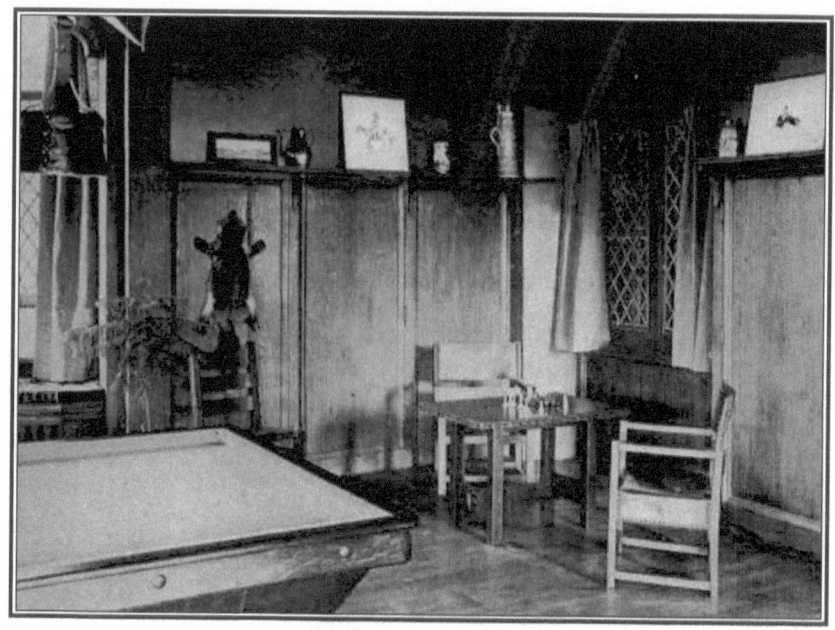

A corner of the Billiard Room of Ernest J. White

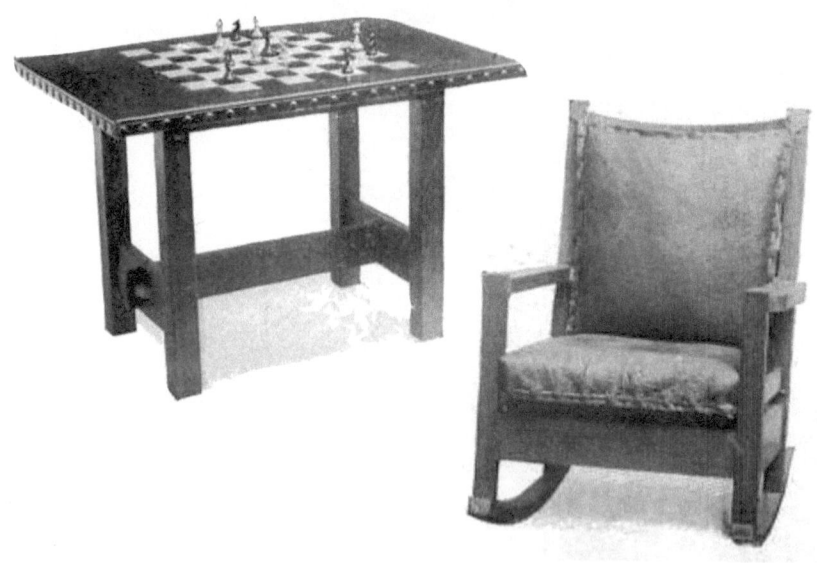

WILLIAM MORRIS

ALTHOUGH the name of William Morris has long since become a household word throughout America, yet the personality of the man, as well as his great part in the world's work, is definitely known but to the few. His was a versatile genius, each phase of which appeals to a more or less extended public.

To students of literature he is an innovator in his art; one who introduced a new element into the Victorian age; a poet who, beginning his career as an Anglo-Norman mediaevalist, next drew inspiration from the Greek and Latin classics, and finally from widened reading, knowledge and travel, absorbed, at first hand, influences from the Scandinavians who peopled Iceland. In literature, William Morris is the enthusiastic student of Chaucer; he is the creator of "The Earthly Paradise;" the modern skald who, learned in language, legend and history, told to English-speaking folk the Great Story of the North, which, in his own opinion, "should be for all our race what the tale of Troy was to the Greeks."

For others, William Morris represents a most important factor in the progress of modern art. He was a member of that group of brilliant, earnest young Englishmen who, at the middle of the Nineteenth Century, revolutionized the national school of painting, and generated a current of aestheticism whose vibrations are still felt, not only in the parent country, but as well in America and in France. From his relations with the Pre-Raphaelite Brotherhood

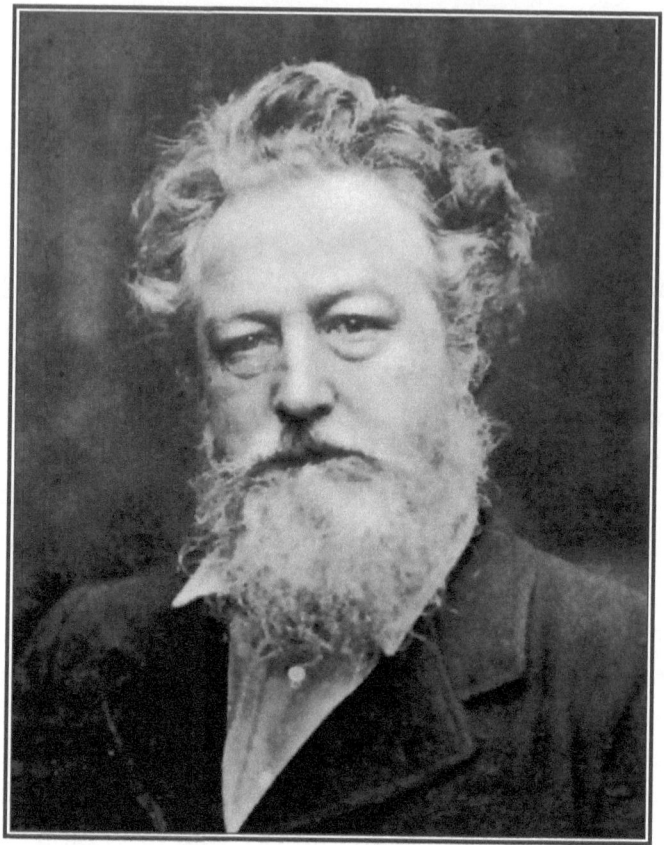

WILLIAM MORRIS

and from his own practical genius, Morris evolved a system of household art, which has largely swept away the ugly and the commonplace from the English middle-class home. He so became an expert in what he himself was pleased to call "the lesser arts of life," He was a handicraftsman, "an artisan self-taught and highly skilled in the technical processes of a half dozen trades" He disdained no apprenticeship however humble, no labor however protracted, arduous and disfiguring, in order that he might become the practical master of his work. The attainments of his genius, of his careful and intelligent study remain as lasting witnesses to the impetus and direction given by him to the arts and crafts of his time.

Again, many who, through ignorance or prejudice, refuse to recognize the functions of literature and art in the economy of life, still regard William Morris as a lost leader, friend and brother. For such as these, he is the man who, by the light of history and of his own conscience, distinctly saw the evils of society as it is at present constituted; who lent his energies, his fortune and his fame to remedy the wrongs of the oppressed masses, and to prepare the advent of the reign of natural law. In William Morris all socialists honor the unprejudiced man of wealth, culture and position, who plainly formulated the proposition that:

"It is right and just that all men should have work to do which shall be worth doing, and be of itself pleasant to do; and which should be done under such conditions as would make it neither over-wearisome nor over-anxious."

Finally, above and beyond each and all of these claims of William Morris to the present and future consideration of the world, there lies the memory of his great heart which so animated all enterprises into which he entered that, at his death, a coworker wrote of him: "Morris was a splendid leader, a great poet, artist and craftsman, a still greater man, and, oh! such a friend to know and love."

The place of Morris among the Victorian poets has been exhaustively treated by critics and reviewers, and it is well known that, at the death of Tennyson, the honors of the Laureate would have been for him an easy victory. His accomplishments in the various arts and crafts to which he successively devoted himself, have been chronicled and criticised from time to time, and in various countries and languages. But it is not generally appreciated that his art and his Socialism were associated integrally with each other, or, rather, that they were but two aspects of the same thing. However, this fact becomes evident to anyone who will follow his life which, in its intellectual aspects, although it was apparently subject to abrupt changes, was, in reality, a logical expansion of inter-dependent ideas.

It is as an artist-socialist that we will briefly consider him.

The traditions of his family surrounded him with conservatism. He was born of affluent parents whose wealth increased during his childhood and youth. His father, a London City banker, gaining a controlling interest in productive copper-mines, grew wealthy beyond his own expectations, and was thus able to afford his children the most desirable educational and social advantages, as also to secure to them, at his own death, a very considerable fortune.

William Morris, the eldest of five sons, was destined for the Church, and for that reason, was entered, at the age of fourteen, at Marlboro College, there to be educated under clerical masters. Even in these early days, the characteristics of the future artist and thinker were most marked and singular. The boy was father to the man. The lax discipline, the weakness of the school organization acted in no unfavorable way upon the scholar whose moral and physical strength gave him a unique place among the student body. Rather, these conditions afforded him opportunity for cultivating his individual tastes and for developing his peculiar powers. The school library at Marlboro was rich in works upon archaeology and ecclesiastical architecture, and through these, with his remarkable power of assimilation, he ranged at will. He there acquired that accurate knowledge, which, further developed by minute examination of all existing monuments, constituted him a great authority upon English Gothic, and, at the same time, a protector of the mediaeval cathedrals and churches against the vandalism of so-called "restorations." A school-fellow at Marlboro describes Morris as one who, given to solitude and monologues, was considered "a little mad" by the other boys: a dreamer who invented and poured forth endless stories of "knights and fairies," in which one adventure rose out of another; the tale flowing on from day to day, throughout a whole term. Another peculiarity then noticeable in him was the restlessness of his fingers. The natural undeveloped craftsman sought an outlet for his manual activity in endless netting. While studying in the large school-room, he worked for hours together, with one end of the net fastened to a desk and his fingers moving automatically. Altogether, the impression made by Morris upon his associates of those days was that of a boy remarkable for his physical force and his intense love of nature, but whose scholarship was quite ordinary, barring his intimate acquaintance with English history and architecture.

Leaving Marlboro, Morris passed under the tutorship of a High Churchman of fine attainment and character, of wide sympathies and of cultivated tastes, which extended to the fine arts. Responsive to the new influences, the boy developed into a more than fair classical scholar, and received the inspiration of the strongly individual literary and artistic work of his future years. But the decisive moment of his life occurred in June, 1852, when on passing his matriculation examination for Exeter College, Oxford, he occupied a desk next to that of Edward Burne-Jones, who was destined to be his life-long and most intimate friend.

Going into residence in what he himself called the most beautiful of the ancient cities of England, the atmosphere of Oxford became for him a forcing-place for that peculiar quality of mediaeval thought and culture, which, in his mature years, permeated his personality and vivified every piece of work, intellectual and manual, proceeding from him. Concerning the gracious influences of the old university town, he wrote late in life:

"There are many places in England where a young man may get as good book-learning as in Oxford; but not one where he can receive the education which the loveliness of the grey city used to give us."

The impulse toward mediaeval was further strengthened in Morris, during his undergraduate days, by a study tour through the cathedral towns of France, notably Rouen and Amiens, as well as by a course of reading which gained him an intimate acquaintance with Froissart and with the Arthurian legends: two wells of thought from whose inexhaustible depths he drew an endless chain of artistic motifs.

The development of his social and political ideas was slower and later than his advancement in literature and art. During his residence at Oxford, he saw no objection to the monarchical principle; but yet, in the abandonment of his purpose to take Holy Orders, we may see the beginning of his revolt against constituted authority. The secularization of his mind, the widening of his interests convinced him that art and literature were not mere handmaidens of religion, but rather interests to be pursued for their own sake; that they were no less than the means of realizing life. For a short period indeed, he had cherished the idea of founding a religious Brotherhood whose patron was to be Sir Galahad of the Arthurian legend, and whose rules should include both celibacy and conventual life. But the idea of a common organized effort toward a higher life, which had been planned by Morris and his group of associates Burne-Jones, Faulkner and others gradually changed from the form of a monastic to that of a social brotherhood. With the passage of years, this socialistic idea expanded in the mind of William Morris, until the feelings which he had first entertained toward a small circle of personal friends extended so as to embrace the world, its work and its interests. Then, he declared himself in revolt against existing authorities; demanding a condition of society in which there should be "neither rich nor poor, neither master nor master's man, neither idle nor overworked, in which all men should live in equality of condition, and would manage their affairs unwastefully, with the full consciousness that harm to one would very well mean harm to all: and also the realization at last of the meaning of the word: COMMONWEALTH."

Such an evolution of thought was a direct result of Morris's study of the art and citizenship of the Middle Ages, just as evidently as his first idea of a religious brotherhood proceeded from an ardent study of the story of the knights of the Round Table. The former fact he acknowledged during the course of a debate on Socialism, which occurred at Cambridge, in 1884. His statement is as follows:

"I have come thoroughly to understand the manner of work under which the art of the Middle Ages was done, and that it is the only manner of work which can turn out popular art; only to discover that it is impossible to work in that manner in this profitgrinding society. So on all sides I am driven toward revolution as the only hope, and I am growing clearer and clearer on the speedy advent of it in a very obvious form."

The successive steps of his study and the specific

accomplishments which gave him claim to the recognition and gratitude of many sorts and conditions of men are interesting and significant. His individuality and fearlessness asserted themselves in his first choice of a profession; for having received his baccalaureate degree, he sorely disappointed his family by binding himself in apprenticeship to an Oxford architect The gravity of this action cannot now be appreciated except by reference to the spirit of the times. The wealthy upper middle classes regarded the men following artistic pursuits as Bohemians: the painters being lowest in the social scale, and the position of architects even being questioned.

At the present distance of time, and in default of documentary evidence, we cannot determine whether it was the archeological, or the artistic faculty in Morris that led him to the choice of a profession. But it would seem to have been the instinct of the born decorator, who understands the relative values of construction and ornament, and who knows that he must first build and afterward beautify. It would seem also that in so choosing, Morris vaguely felt that by force of his commanding intellectual, moral and personal influence, he was destined to redeem and to elevate the then denationalized English decorative arts.

The apprenticeship of Morris as an architect lasted only nine months, but during that time, with the great gift of concentration which characterized him, he gained a knowledge of both principle and detail which would have required a long laborious application from an ordinarily gifted person. His attainments as a builder were never put to extensive practical use, and even on planning his first home, in 1859, the "Red House," at Upton, County Kent, he employed the services of his friend and fellow-student in architecture, Philip Webb; although the latter did little else than to carry out Morris's directions, especially in the design of the interior and its furnishings. The Red House proved to be an epoch-making building. It is remarkable as being the first example of the revived artistic use of red brick in domestic architecture. "The Studio" has referred to it as "that wonderful red building which became the prototype of all the charming houses of the so-called 'Queen Anne.' revival; although it may be said in passing, that it is almost entirely Gothic, with a strong French influence apparent" Finally, it is known mat the household decorative arts for which England became so famous in the latter part of the nineteenth century, grew out of the desire of Morris to provide a suitable home for his lovely bride, and his avowed effort to make that home the most beautiful dwelling-place in the kingdom.

Through the exercise of his ingenuity in mural and ceiling ornamentation, in embroidery design, and in other artistic mediums, he acquired practical experience as a decorator. And from these beginnings grew the work which engaged him from that time forward until his death. The activity consequent upon the planning and furnishing of the "Red House" followed upon a mood of idleness, not infrequent in Morris's youth; but with the coming of the new interests, the tendencies of earlier years disappeared. The eagerness of the maker, the joy of craftsmanship seized him, never to relax their hold. And the dreams of a monastic Brotherhood which had been the constant accompaniment of his Oxford days, evolved into the definite idea of a company of artists pledged to produce beautiful things.

Such was the origin of the firm of Morris & Company, which, beside the chief who devoted to its success his extraordinary talents, his time and his fortune, included among its members other men of genius and great attainment: Madox Brown, whose high place in English painting stands to-day acknowledged; Dante Gabriele Rossetti, who united in himself the incongruous qualities of the idealist, the artist and the astute financier; Burne-Jones, who did most to perpetuate and ennoble the English Pre-Raphaelite tradition; Philip Webb, the builder, as we know, of the "Red House," the master of proportion and ornament, whether as applied to the larger masses of architecture, or yet to small objects of interior decoration; and finally Faulkner, less gifted artistically than the others, but who was a forthright craftsman, a valuable associate as an expert accountant, and whose loyalty and longing for his friends had drawn him from his mathematical tutorship at Oxford to take up the restless life of London.

It is certain that no other such firm has ever been organized; since it was composed of Oxford graduates of distinction, and artists of already high reputation; since, also, its commercial object was wholly subordinate to the interests of art. The main employment of the Company was, at first, ecclesiastical decoration, as the so-called aesthetic revival was then in progress among the London churches. This movement, which was entailed by the vigorous study of history made by the High-Church party, created a demand for mural decoration, stained glass, tiles, carving, metal work and altar embroideries, all of which, by reason of the peculiar talents and tendencies of Burne-Jones, Morris, Brown and Faulkner, could be most intelligently supplied. In the decade 1860-1870, the Morris firm executed windows for Salisbury Cathedral, and for certain of the College churches at Oxford and Cambridge; which works are to-day objects of pilgrimage for those interested in the modern revival of one of the most beautiful of the arts of the Middle Ages. At the same time, very successful experiments in tapestry-weaving and cabinet-making were in progress, as may be learned from the report of the jury of awards at the International Exhibition of 1862. This report, referring to the objects of household art shown by the Morris firm, declares that "the general forms of the furniture, the arrangement of the tapestry, and the character of the details are satisfactory to the archeologist from the exactness of the imitation, at the same time mat the general effect is excellent."

It is needless to trace the development of the Firm at length; since the results of its work may be measured by anyone who has the means to compare the household art of England and America, as it stands today, with the ugliness and barrenness of the upper and middle class homes of those countries, forty years ago. But it must be remembered that to the Firm capital, invention and control were supplied practically by Morris alone. His architectural instinct, the quality in which by his unique strength, built up the material fortunes of the Company from the merest financial nothing, at the same time that it assured the complete aesthetic success of the enterprise by carrying the arts of design to their highest form.

As the desire for beautiful surroundings spread from ecclesiastical into secular life, the call for increased and diversified production made heavy demands upon Morris's time, strength and financial resources. But his energies and his spirit of self-sacrifice never failed or flagged. He was always persistent, sagacious and industrious. In order to revive the arts and crafts which so beautified the otherwise strenuous life of the Middle Ages, he made the most practical and costly experiments in dyeing, weaving and printing. In the exercise of the first of these crafts, he supplemented all that could be learned from books and from chemical tests in his own vats by a thorough apprenticeship among the dyers of Staffordshire. And the results of his Tabor justified the means which he so ungrudgingly employed; for he succeeded in raising to an unexpected degree of beauty, the art which, since the introduction of the anilines at about the middle of the nineteenth century, had fallen into deplorable decline. As a colorist, Morris takes rank among the great masters. He followed the best traditions of Oriental art; using but few elements and obtaining his effects by skillfully varied juxtaposition and contrast. His system of color has been somewhat misunderstood by both buyers and imitators; for the peacock-blues, olive-greens and rusty reds dominant in the stage setting of "Patience" and other satires upon the "Aesthetic Craze," were simply provisional colors used during the early years of the Firm, and set aside by the establishment of the Morris dyehouse, where full frank hues of indigo blue, madder red and weld yellow were perfected, and employed in the production of the beautiful Hammersmith carpets and Merton tapestries and chintzes.

In textile fabrics the progress made by Morris was no less sure and rapid than in the art and craft which we have just considered. His appreciation of necessities and how to accomplish them was alike in all fields of practical work. His attainments in the weaving of tapestry are especially remarkable and characteristic. He criticised the Gobelins Factories as having degraded a "fine art" into a mere "upholsterer's toy," and therefore set himself to revive the craft. In default of any existing instance where the actual weaving process might be observed, Morris gathered details, as best he might, from an old French official handbook, published prior to the Revolution. He caused a handloom to be set up in his own bedroom at Kelmscott House, Hammersmith, and, in order that the new interest should not interfere with his ordinary occupations, he was accustomed to practise weaving in the early morning hours. He so gradually became an expert workman, and even devised technical improvements upon the French historical system. Indeed, he may be said to have restored the splendid and almost extinct art of the fifteenth and sixteenth centuries. This statement is justified by the beautiful works in arras: "The Star of Bethlehem," and the series illustrating "The Quest of the San Graal," designed for the great dining-room of Stanmore Hall, near Harrow.

A third art—that of printing—to the practice of which Morris devoted much time during the later years of his life, would seem at first to be removed from the sphere of the pure decorator. But we find the secret of this devotion in the words of the artist himself: "The only work of art which surpasses a complete mediaeval book is a complete mediaeval building." And hence we realize that here again the architectural instinct provided impulse and energy.

As Morris had realized early in life the impossibility of raising buildings worthy to compare with mediaeval structures, and had found the cause of such impossibility to lie in the adverse circumstances under which the modern workman is compelled to labor, deprived of pleasure in the work of his hands, so the greathearted reformer and artist set himself to remedy the wrong, and to restore the lost pleasure to the worker. His architectural studies led him to Socialism, and when his hopes of effecting great improvements in the economic conditions of his country passed away, he was thrown back upon his own resources to impress his convictions upon the world. So the establishment of his printing-press at Kelmscott Manor, coincides with his withdrawal from active Socialism. Again, his power of quick absorption and assimilation made him a past master of the craft, in which he was also aided by his previous hand-illumination of favorite poems, and his studies in wood-engraving.

The Kelmscott Press created printing as a fine art in England and America, popularized good design in book-covers, and produced a series of beautiful books, the finest of which, the great folio edition of Chaucer, was a tribute of Morris to the literary guide and master of his youth. In the full activity of his labor as printer and publisher, death overtook him; but not before he had drawn the portrait of the ideal handicraftsman, in whom we recognize his own likeness.

"The true workman," he says, "must put his own individual intelligence and enthusiasm into the goods which he fashions. He must have a natural aptitude for his work so strong that no education can force him away from his special bent. He must be "allowed to think of what he is doing, and to vary his work as the circumstances of it vary, and his own moods. He must be forever stirring to make the piece at which he is at work better than the last. He must refuse at anybody's bidding to turn out, I won't say a bad, but even an indifferent piece of work, whatever the public wants, or thinks it wants. He must have a voice, and a voice worth listening to, in the whole affair."

The production of this skilled handicraftsman was, in Morris's belief, an ideal not beyond realization. His system was that of setting the nearest person to do whatever work needed to be done. He preferred general intelligence to innate manual dexterity. He inveighed against that excessive division of labor which cramps and sterilizes the modern artificer. He demanded a knowledge of drawing as the basis of all manual arts and as an essential element of a general education which should be worthy of the name. In a word, he sought to unite the artist and the workman in one person, and thus to prevent the making of designs which the designer can not produce with his own hands.

Although the artistic principles of Morris have been questioned, it is acknowledged that personally he made them successful. In his own case, he did not divorce practice and theory; since to his immense production of designs, which in textile fabrics alone numbered more than six hundred, he added the experience of a thorough craftsman. Furthermore, he did not allow his own interests and occupations, absorbing and exacting though they were, to blind him to the larger questions of the hour, in which he could be of service to his country, his century and the world; as is evidenced by his action and prominence in the Society for the Preservation of Ancient Buildings, and by the fearless enthusiasm with which he disseminated Socialistic propaganda. He laid down no empty formulas, and like his master Chaucer's "Poure Parson," first he wrought, and afterward he taught. As we have before said, his art and his Socialism were one and inseparable; for he entered upon his political course blankly ignorant of economics and in the effort to make possible for the workman "a life to which the perception and creation of beauty, the enjoyment of real pleasure that is, shall be felt to be as necessary as daily bread." Like Karl Marx, he seemed to believe that the relations of man to man have formed an ascending evolutionary series, developed through the successive organic periods of history, and that they are now undergoing a last crisis, at whose end, these relations having been those of master and slave in the ancient republics, lord and serf in the Middle Ages, capitalist and laborer in the nineteenth century, shall ultimately, under the happy reign of Socialism, become those of brother and brother.

WILLIAM MORRIS

WILLIAM MORRIS
HIS SOCIALISTIC CAREER.

EDITOR'S NOTE—in the effort to offer an accurate portratt-sketch of William Morris, the artist-socialist, handicraftsman, poet and man of business, we have thought best not to conceal those characteristics which separated him so widely from the men of his class and condition. The force and even vehemence of his nature led him to extremes which are inconceivable to the calm-minded and conservative.

But in his violent and sudden reversions from the active to the contemplative life, we may see the effort of a truly practical man of his time to control the impulse of the prophet within him, who looked forward to a distant age when all social wrongs should be righted, and the relations of man to man should be those of brother to brother.

We present the personality of William Morris with neither praise nor blame; but simply with the suggestion that if we take him for all in all, we shall not soon see his like again.

SOCIALISM is a word often vaguely and indiscriminately used; since its definition differs greatly in the various groups of those who profess its principles. Therefore, in order to understand the methods of thought and action of any individual classing himself among those seeking a re-adjustment of the present relations between man and man, it is necessary to discover the germ-ideas of the individual, and to consider the environment which forced these ideas into development and productiveness.

In the case of William Morris, the evolution is most interesting, in that it presents a slow, natural, normal process, divided into the three phases observed in all living things: a weak infancy; a vigorous maturity; a troubled and passive decline. From documentary evidence, we learn that in youth Morris had no objection to the principle of monarchy. Indeed, his undergraduate utterances in the Oxford and Cambridge Magazine (which was founded by himself and his Exeter College friends) have a true Carlylian ring, when he says:

"People will have a king, a leader of some sort, after all: wherein they are surely right, only I wish they would not choose king critic-mob."

The passage quoted was written in 1856, when Morris was as yet the country-bred boy, the easy liver and aristocrat. But the influence of certain of his college associates was like seed left to germinate in his mind. His friends, Price and Faulkner, brought to Oxford actual knowledge of the inhuman conditions of human life in the great industrial areas of England. Their practical enthusiasm for Factory Acts, for sanitation, for all that implied the betterment of the condition of the working classes gradually replaced in the mind of Morris what we may call his personal Mediaevalism; that is: the tendency to excessive hero-worship, and the desire to isolate himself from the common life of the world. He came very slowly to recognize that the classes, or strata of society are interdependent; that harm to one means harm to all; that true freedom, real mon and living art depend upon the physical and social being of the masses.

Morris's stage of development at the outbreak of the Russo-Turkish War, which proved to be a crisis in his life, may be described as nothing beyond a frank and thorough liberalism; but yet the trend of his evolution as a thinker was then plainly visible. This moment has been called by one of his most sympathetic biographers: "The Parting of the Ways," It was the beginning of his conversion to a definite and dogmatic socialism. The occasion can be briefly described.

In the autumn of 1876, England was stirred by the reports of Turkish massacres in Bulgaria, and public opinion rallied to the Russian and Christian side; but, during the course of a few weeks, the influence of the Tory ministry so changed the dominant sentiment that the country seemed about to take up arms in the cause of Turkey. Then it was that William Morris, hitherto known only as an artist and literary man, addressed his now famous letter to "The London Daily News," under the caption: "England and the Turks." After scathing the authors of the Bulgarian massacres and the party in England which, for political and commercial reasons, was ready to condone them, Morris declared that the Tories, in case they precipitated the country into defending the Turks, would find only shame in victory. He ended by an appeal to the working men, recognizing them, for the first time, as an organized body struggling toward clearer light and higher ground. For a final sarcasm, he begged to inscribe himself, in company with Gladstone, Freeman the historian, and all other men whom he esteemed, as "a hysterical sentimentalist"

The war-party persisted in its efforts, and to meet the political crisis, the Eastern Question Association was formed by the friends of neutrality and peace. For a meeting called in the interests of this organization, in January 1878, Morris composed a song in support of the object of the meeting, and beginning with the words: "Wake, London Lads." Collaborating with the patriot-poet, Burne-Jones, the artist designed a platform ticket bearing a vignette entitled: "Blind War." It is interesting to know that both these unusual souvenirs are extant; being preserved in a volume of documents bearing upon the Eastern Question.

Morris had now in middle life shown himself keenly sensitive to the problems of modern civilization. Through a deep study of mediaeval art and citizenship, he had come to be a Socialist in the true sense: not a propagandist and a destructive agent, but rather one who regarded his fellow-beings in some degree as companions, and who ceased not to advocate equity, good-will and kindness. In defining the Socialism of Morris, a well-known American critic has said: "It grew out of his love of art, which inflamed him to bring all men within its domain." And so it would appear; since according to his own testimony, and that of his friends and biographers, he entered upon his socialistic career ignorant of economics; to which study he afterward devoted much good-will, and, at times, it must be confessed, ill-directed although sincere efforts.

From the conditions of its origin and early development, the Socialism of William Morris was always largely free from doctrine and dogma. It was innate in his being, through his complete understanding of the principles from which a free life and a pure art can alone spring. As formulated in his mind, it was a system which would abolish, entirely, or in great part, the individual effort and competition on which modern society rests, and substitute for it co-operative action; which would introduce a more perfect and equal distribution of the products of labor, and would make land and capital, as the instruments and means of production, the joint possession of the members of the community.

With such beliefs as these, Morris set himself to denounce with pen and voice the modern industrial and economic system. From the platform of the Hall of University College, Oxford, he cried out to the undergraduates before him: "It is my business here tonight and everywhere to foster your discontent," and as a practical step toward a new order of society, he counseled the young men to marry beneath their station, in order to break down the existing barriers between class and class.

Protests arose against the defection of the man of position, wealth and education from the class into which he was born. Certain of his acquaintances, and among them even those who knew him well, regarded his Socialism as a sudden, unreasonable, inexplicable action. To such as these always remained unknown the long struggle, the deep brooding, the hesitations and the discouragements through which Morris passed during his career as a Socialist. Accustomed to find his thoughts and actions misconstrued by those who, with little pains, might have understood them, he realized his loneliness with a touching pathos: "I have had a life of insults." he once said.

Again, in a private letter, he wrote on New Year's Day, 1881:

"I have of late been somewhat melancholy. When one is just so much subdued, one is apt to turn more specially from thinking of one's own affairs to more worthy matters; and my mind is very full of the great change, which I hope, is slowly coming over the world. Nor will you perhaps think it ceremonious or superstitious, if I try to join thoughts with you today in writing a word of hope for the new year; that it may do a good turn of work toward the abasement of the rich and the raising up of the poor, which is of all things most to be longed for; till people can, at last, rub out from their dictionaries altogether these dreadful words: RICH and POOR."

Four years later, a sense of despair seems to have stolen over him, after one of his visits to the East End of London. He writes:

"On Sunday, I went a-preaching Stepney way. My visit intensely depressed me, as these Eastward visits always do; the mere stretch of houses, the vast mass of utter shabbiness and uneventfulness, sits upon one like a nightmare. You would perhaps have smiled at my congregation; some twenty people in a little room...It is a great drawback that I can't talk to them roughly and unaffectedly. I don't seem to have got at them yet you see this GREAT CLASS GULF lies between us."

In the effort to make plain the intense, lonely and lofty personality of William Morris, we are, perhaps, losing sight of his evolution as a Socialist. We have seen that the Eastern Question, in its phase of 1876-1878, was the active cause of his conversion to the faith in which he died. When he entered upon his novitiate, by his own confession, he had not so much as opened Adam Smith's "Wealth of Nations" which for Englishmen is the Genesis of economics. Nor had he even heard of Ricardo or Karl Marx. His Socialism from the beginning was of the heart, not of the head. Through the same rapid power of absorption and assimilation which caused mm to master successively a half dozen arts and crafts, he gained a theoretic knowledge of the political and social principles which he adopted midway in life. As understood by him, Socialism represented those hopes of the laboring classes which had been extinguished more than a quarter-century previously by the collapse of the movement known as Chartism: which demanded recognition by the government of the citizenship and the human rights of the working man.

A public profession of faith was made by Morris in joining the so-called Social Democratic Federation, which rose in 1883 out of the union of the Radical, or Liberal clubs of London: these being organizations whose object was to advocate the reform and control of Parliament by making its members habitually subservient to their constituents. The rise of the Federation marked the first appearance in England of modern, or scientific Socialism, and the first step of the new body was to institute a series of meetings for the discussion of "Practical Remedies for Pressing Needs;" the subjects including the now familiar "Eight Hours Law," "Free Meals for School Children," and the "Nationalization of Railways." In the first discussion Morris participated, and his adhesion to the body, because of his high character and great reputation, was counted as a notable victory for the cause. Indeed, so important was it regarded, that a prominent Socialist cried out:

"It has doubled our strength at a single stroke!"

The programme of the Democratic Federation to which Morris subscribed was virtually a scheme of State Socialism; that is: the joint ownership by all members of the State of the land, and of the instruments and means of production; the distribution among the members of the produce, by a public act, performed according to rules laid down by the State; the negation of ownership on part of the members of the State of things that do not perish in the using. To these theories, distant from their accomplishment, were joined practical measures for the betterment of the condition of the working man, and for the extinction of competition. Toward the evils of the modern commercial system Morris was especially bitter. He describes the artisans of to-day as "working consciously for a livelihood, and blindly for a mere abstraction of a world-market, but with no thought of the wares passing through their hands."

With these human automata he thus compares the craftsmen of the Middle Ages:

"Who worked directly for their neighbors, understanding their wants, and with no middle men coming between them."

"Now," he continues, "people work under the direction of an absolute master whose power is restrained by a trade's union, in absolute hostility to that master. In the Middle Ages, they worked under the direction of their own collective wills by means of trade guilds. The old system, in its simplicity, assumed that commerce was made for man; whereas our modem system is based on the assumption that man is made for commerce; that he is not an intelligent being; but a machine, or part of a machine that yields but one result: the degradation of the external surroundings of life, or, simply and plainly: UNHAPPINESS."

The work of Morris in the interests of the Federation (and it was arduous and long continued) is very well indicated by the titles of four lectures which he delivered in the large towns of the United Kingdom: "Useful Work versus Useless Toil;" "Art and Labor;" "Misery and the Way Out of It;" "How we Live and How we Might Live."

The loyalty of the great man to the Federation and its interests was limitless; but the Socialism of the body rapidly assumed a dogmatic and sectarian coloring. Toward the end of 1884, a rupture occurred in the organization, and Morris was the most important and influential figure among the seceders; since the broad-minded patriot and humanitarian revolted against the assertion that a Socialist, worthy of the name, could not live and work outside the Federation. A new club, or body, "The Socialistic League," of which Morris was the treasurer, was now formed, with the purpose of promoting Revolutionary International Socialism. An official journal of the League was immediately founded, and its first issue, under the name of "The Commonweal," opened with an introductory column, written and signed by Morris, which was in advance of any socialistic sentiments previously expressed by him. In the course of the article, he observed:

"It is our duty to attack unsparingly the miserable system which would make all civilization end in a society of rich and poor, of skves and slave-owners." And again: "We assume as a matter of course that a government of privileged persons, hereditary and commercial, cannot act usefully toward the community. Their position forbids it Their arrangements for the distribution of the plunder of the workers, their struggles for the national share of the exploitation of barbarous peoples are nothing to us, except so far as they may give us an opportunity for instilling Socialism into their minds."

The League advocated the complete destruction of existing social conditions; offering as a substitute a State in which land, capital, machinery, factories, workshops, means of transit, mines, banking, and all means of producing and distributing wealth should be declared the common property of all.

During a membership in the League of six years (1884-1890), Morris was unwearied in his efforts as a writer and public speaker, and generous to the point of lavishness with his private contributions to the expenses of the body. Two hundred fifty issues of "The Commonweal" passed through his hands; lectures were delivered by him in all parts of the Kingdom, irrespective of weather and personal comfort; his superb collection of early printed books was sacrificed to the cause that he loved; and, following his other treasures, his health was thrown ungrudgingly into the balance.

In 1887, at the culmination of the acute stage of his Socialism, Morris took part in the gathering ordered to assemble in the Trafalgar Square, and to be composed of delegates from the Radical Clubs of London, the Irish National League, the Democratic Federation and the Socialistic League. A spectator has thus graphically described the demonstration, as the great concourse of people began to pour out of the Square, down Parliament Street:

"On they came, with a sort of irresistible force, and right in front among the red flags, singing with all his might, was William Morris. He had the face of a Crusader, and he marched as the Crusaders must have marched."

As in the case of the first organization, narrow and dangerous tendencies developed within the Socialistic League which drifted toward Communist-Anarchism. While thus his companions were restive of all authority, Morris, although believing in a complete equality of condition for all persons, insisted that there must be a public, or social conscience, to restrain the desires and passions of individuals; without which Authority there could be no Society.

So, once again, Morris found himself detached from those whom he had chosen as companions in social progress, and in 1890, in his farewell article in "The Commonweal," he acknowledged that the ideals for which he had so fervently labored, and which at times had seemed to him so near of realization, were distant and impalpable. He retired to write his most important and mature work upon the great movement, which he gave to the world under the title of "Socialism, Its Growth and Outcome." For the remaining years of his fife he was passive in the cause. He recognized that the accumulated wrongs of centuries cannot be set right in a lifetime; that the evolution of human happiness cannot be otherwise than very gradual.

THE FIRM OF
MORRIS & COMPANY, DECORATORS.

THIS firm, by reason of its peculiar constitution, stands unique in the history of business ventures. Forty years since, had its scheme been offered to practical men of affairs, it would have been rejected with sarcasm and ridicule. Even now to the prudent-minded, a similar enterprise would seem to be lacking in the elements which assure success. Two features of its organization call for special comment. Firstly: It was composed of artists, students and literary men whose aspirations and occupations drew them away from the method of the shop and the counting-room. Secondly: It was founded for the production of objects demanding the highest originality of conception and the most accomplished skill in execution, upon a capital which was merely nominal.

The idea of the Firm rose almost equally from two impulses on the part of its members: the desire for an intimate association together, which should extend to all the concerns of life; the desire also to furnish and decorate a single house which was to be the permanent home of William Morris.

In undergraduate days at Oxford, Morris and Burne-Jones had devised a religious brotherhood in which they both hoped to live, cloistered and as celibates. But as their thought was gradually secularized by years and by London experiences, they came to realize that the demand of modern times is for work and not meditation. So, the dream of the monastery condensed into a real workshop, and the brothers of the religious order evolved into handicraftsmen. The house built for Morris by his friend and fellow-student in architecture, Philip Webb, was completed as to its work in brick and wood in 1859. But owing to what has been called by a critic: "The flat ugliness of the current article," the owner and his group of artist-friends set themselves to the designing of the house furnishings and utensils; from the tables, cupboards and settles down to the fire-dogs, candlesticks and table-glass.

The success attendant upon these efforts was recognized at its practical and possible value; and the idea of the firm, as it would now appear, occurred simultaneously to a number of the prospective members; the two oldest and best-known artists of the group, Rossetti and Ford Madox Brown, having the largest share in establishing the enterprise; while it must be acknowledged that the permanence of the work and influence was due alone to the patience, energy, enthusiasm and originality of William Morris.

The firm was called into existence in April, 1861, and an assessment was made of one pound sterling per share; one share being held by each member. This scanty sum and an unsecured loan of one hundred pounds from Mrs. Morris, mother of the artist, furnished the trading capital for the first year.

The initial step of the new association was to make its existence known to the public, by means of a circular letter which, by reason of its style and contents, awakened much comment, antagonism and even ridicule. At this period, the practice of the decorative arts was generally understood to be a superficial accomplishment best suited to affluent young ladies; and the current opinion of the tradesman was such that no person of culture and position would lightly subject himself to the reproach of having sold his birthright. Indeed, the prejudice excited by the circular can scarcely be appreciated at the present time. Nor did the bitter opposition come from one quarter alone. The tradesmen themselves resented the intrusion into their affairs of a body of men whose training had not been commercial, and whose influence, they foresaw, would be destructive to their system.

The effect of this pressure from without was to consolidate the membership of the firm, to kindle the common enthusiasm, and to establish a healthful freedom of criticism between the employers and the employed. The situation was a novel one, and as the work was carried farther and farther afield, the ideals rose to heights which were, at the beginning, unsuspected by the boldest member of the friendly circle.

The original intentions of the Firm are best understood by reference to the circular letter, and as this is become an historical document, quotations from it are of real significance to those interested in the development of the decorative arts. The composition of the letter bears traces of what has been called "the imperious accent" of Rossetti; but, as we know, after events more than justified the initial claims made by the artists.

The letter is headed by the first title of the Firm:

"Morris, Marshall, Faulkner & Company, Fine Art Workmen in Painting, Carving, Furniture and the Metals;" and the names of the members follow in alphabetical order.

The document then proceeds: "The growth of decorative art in this country has now reached a point at which it seems desirable that artists of reputation should devote their time to it Although no doubt particular instances of success may be cited, still it must be generally felt that attempts of this kind hitherto have been crude and fragmentary. Up to this time, the want of that artistic supervision, which can alone bring about harmony between the various parts of a successful work has been increased by the necessarily excessive outlay consequent upon taking one individual artist from his pictorial labors."

After enlarging upon the advantages of association and co-operation, and having enumerated the classes of objects to be produced by the Firm, the letter ends with the subjoined concise paragraph, the sentiment of which is worthy to serve as a text for those who preach the gospel of household art: "It is only requisite to state further that work of all the above classes will be estimated for, and executed in a business-like manner; and it is believed that good decoration involving rather the luxury of taste than the luxury of costliness will be found much less expensive than is generally supposed."

This last statement was abundantly proven by the accomplishments of the Morris Firm, or rather by those of Morris himself, who wrought a silent revolution in the most necessary arts and crafts, and whose influence having beautified the English middle-class home, gradually involved the New World in the movement toward true aestheticism.

If we follow the history of the Firm, we find that, at the beginning of the year 1862, the organization was in full working order. A further call was at that time made of nineteen pounds sterling (one share representing each member); thus raising the paid-in capital to one hundred forty pounds, which was never increased till the dissolution of the firm in 1874. A few hundred pounds of further capital was supplied by loans, which bore, or were supposed to bear, interest at five per cent.; these loans coming from Morris himself, or from his mother. Work done for the firm by any member was credited to his account at fixed rates, and paid, like other debts; while Morris, as general manager, received a salary of one hundred fifty pounds.

After the manner of all artistic enterprises, the Firm passed through many crises and led for several years a true Bohemian existence. Production was necessarily slow, as it was the result of experiment and venture. Sales were uncertain, since the effort of production was doubled by the task of creating an intelligent purchasing public. And, hardest of all, there was no reserve fund upon which to draw. The extension of the business, although finally remunerative, at times unbalanced the finances, and Morris, little by little, cast his entire fortune into the rapidly developing scheme. But owing to his industry, sagacity and constancy, the Firm survived, and a capital began to form itself from the accumulated profits. These last were, in strict law, and according to the first contract, equally divisible among the partners who, it is needless to say, bore very unequal shares in the labor of designing and executing; none beside Morris and Faulkner devoting their exclusive time to the affairs of the company. Hence, through the initial fault of the enterprise, arose unpleasant complications which impaired and even destroyed friendships, and nearly led to disaster, at the time of the dissolution and reconstitution of the Firm in 1874.

As the Company extended its activities, which were at first largely confined to the production of household furniture and stained glass, Morris was subjected to the sarcasm of Rossetti. "Top has taken to worsted work" wrote the Chief of the Pre-Raphaelites; using the familiar name applied to Morris by his intimates, as a shortened form of Topsy, and as indicating his thick mop of hair. The "worsted work," or rather embroidery in crewels, was applied to dark serge of Yorkshire manufacture, and designed for mural decoration. In after years, this material with its applied ornament, was superseded by the chintzes and paper-hangings which became the staple products of the Firm. Still later, were developed the beautiful carpets and tapestries upon which Morris lavished the best efforts of his study and manual skill, as well as a wealth of time and physical strength.

Midway in the sixties, the fortunes of the Firm improved with the spread of Ritualism; owing to which movement commissions for church decoration were received in great number; BurneJones, Madox Brown and Morris furnishing cartoons for stained glass, and Morris alone the designs for hangings, altar-cloths and floor tiles.

The work of the Firm thus rapidly increasing, and the original workshops in Red Lion Square, W. C proving insufficient, the question of removal became imperative. It was first proposed to make additions to the Red House at Upton, so that Burne-Jones as well as Morris might live there, and to locate the new workshops in the vicinity of the beautiful residence. But this plan was rejected because of the distance of the place from London, and the difficulty of country travel in stormy and wintry weather. Then Morris found himself forced to choose between giving up the home, which he had hoped to make the most artistic house in England, and the alternative of retiring from the Company into which he had put so much of his best thought and work. He chose the latter course, and did further violence to his feelings by renting a house in Queen Square, Bloomsbury, large enough to serve as both living place and workshops. From the Red House he retired in the autumn of 1865; leaving behind him splendid art-treasures which were too cumbrous for displacement, or else by their very nature unremovable. Such were the mural paintings in tempera executed by Burne-Jones; the sideboard designed by Philip Webb; and the two great cupboards, the one painted with "The Marriage of King Rene;" the other with the story of the Niebelungenlied. The Red House Morris never saw again, since, as he acknowledged, the experience would have been too painful for him. The new home in Queen Square was not altogether without dignity, as it was situated in the fashionable suburb of the London of Queen Anne and bore distinct marks of its old-time splendor.

For the next five years, Morris lived and labored in London; devoting the time saved by combining his workshops and residence to technical experiments and to new literary studies. During this period, the business affairs of Morris & Company were directed by a Mr. Taylor, a man of artistic taste and financial ability, under whom the Firm became organized and prosperous. These years were also marked by the receipt of the first really important commission in non-ecclesiastical decorative work: the mural decoration of the Green Dining Room at the South Kensington Museum, which today remains intact, and which, although of heavy first cost, is now regarded by the Museum authorities as the most economical outlay ever made upon the buildings. The work, from its singular merit, proved to be of great value in making known the name of the Firm and the specific character of its productions. As is usual, success engendered success, and the business extended so rapidly as even to cause anxiety among the members of the Company. As we have seen. the capital, invention and control were supplied practically by Morris, who, nevertheless, under the original instrument of the partnership. could not claim greater rights in the management of the assets of the Firm than any of his five or six associates. On the other hand, the members whose connection with the Firm was slight, might, at any moment, find themselves seriously involved in the liabilities of the business, which had been established prior to the passage of the Limited Company Act. The profits, after the first year or two, and for several reasons, had never been divided. But these legal claims now represented sums which involved intricate calculations, and which, if settled, would drain the resources of the business, that is to say: the private fortune of William Morris.

The question of dissolution having been discussed, three of the partners: Burne-Jones, Faulkner and Webb, refused to accept any consideration in respect to their claims as partners; while the other three stood for the strict letter of their legal rights. The position of the latter group is explained in the words of an attorney: "That as in the inception of the Firm no member invested money, nor gave any time or labor, without being paid at an agreed rate, the position of the several members ought to be considered as equal in respect to their claims on the assets of the Firm; further, the good will ought to be taken at three years' purchase and ought to be included in the said assets."

The extreme falsity of such claims is manifest; since the associates, other than Morris, and beyond the first assessment, had contributed nothing toward the capital They had also, as they averred, been paid on every occasion when they had given assistance, or furnished designs or other work to the Company; by which arrangement Morris, in all justice, was released from obligations toward them. But the usual contest between law and equity ensued Long and complicated negotiations were made on one side and the other. Friendships were broken, and among them, that of Rossetti with Morris was never again renewed. Finally, the dissolution was effected, but without satisfaction to the contestants, and a new firm came into existence in March, 1875, bearing the name of Morris & Company, and under the sole management and proprietorship of William Morris; Burne-Jones and Webb retiring their interests, but continuing to aid with designs for stained glass and furniture.

At last, the world's verdict repaired the injuries inflicted by friends upon the upright man and the great artist Morris is today honored in England, France and America as a personality unique in the nineteenth century, and as one who practised the most essential arts and crafts only to transfigure them.

WILLIAM MORRIS

THE OPERA OF ⟩ PATIENCE ⟨
AND
⟩ THE AESTHETIC MOVEMENT ⟨

A QUARTER-CENTURY since, the Gilbert-Sullivan Operas were at the height of their barrel-organ fame. But it was impossible tnen to decide upon their permanent value. Now, at the present distance of time, these lively satires upon political abuses, art movements and social vagaries possess a distinct value as historical documents. The generation which has arisen since they were composed, gains through them a more rapid and vital understanding of the times which they satirize than it were possible to do through the medium of histories and biographies alone. For to these, by reason of their dramatic form, they stand in the relation of people to books. From this point of view, the most valuable of them all is "Patience," the overcharged picture of the aesthetic movement of 1870-1880. In this case, as always, the very exaggeration of the caricature betrays the power of the thing caricatured. Bunthorne and Archibald are ridiculous and grotesque only because they represent the perversion of qualities, culture and grace wnich might, but for the bias of the individual, have been very real and very forceful. The "aesthetic maidens" whose rhythmic movements and utterances are followed by such spontaneous laughter from the auditory, may be classified with literary parodies and travesties which are successful in the degree that they offer a sharp contrast with the beauty of the original work.

The key-note of the aesthetic movement was sincerity. The foible held up to ridicule in "Patience" is affectation: "My mediaevalism is not real," confesses in a burst of confidence the arch-pretender who momentarily is freed from his devotees. "I love you with a fourteenth-century Florentine frenzy" is another declaration whose alliterative catchiness conceals a deeper meaning than is suspected by the many who applaud it With an "airy word" dropped here and there, "Patience" vitalizes the history of the revolution effected in the externals of English middle-class life by Ruskin, Pre-Raphaelitism and all that this term implies.

The aesthetic movement was far from being superficial; nor was it even confined to a single branch of interest It arose from roots hidden deeply in English thought and life. It was perhaps Walter Scott who, in his romances, first displayed a real mediaevalism. when he dared, in the face of an effete classic art to assert and glorify the majestic beauty of Gothic architecture. Next came the Anglo-Catholic movement at Oxford. which although culminating in 1845 with the secession of John Newman to the Roman Church, continued long afterward to be a prodigious force; restoring to English churches and church services some part of their original beauty and symbolism, and thence carrying into secular life a love of the Fine Arts. which were regarded in the Middle Ages as the handmaidens of religion. Another source of the aesthetic movement is found in the writings of Ruskin, which became for the Pre-Raphaelites a new gospel and a fixed creed. Finally, the direct cause of the art movement must be recognized in the powerful and self-centered personality of Gabriel Rossetti, who drew after him and, for a time, molded as he willed, the two younger men, Morris and Burne-Jones. the real and effective workers in the Pre-Raphaelite, or aesthetic movement. These three friends. together with Hotnan Hunt. John Everett Millais and Madox Brown, laid the foundations for the present eminence of English art, pictorial and decorative.

In 1821, John Constable predicted that within thirty years the art of his nation would have ceased to exist. Later, in the forties, Ruskin recorded that the Royal Academy Exhibitions repeated again and again: "The same foolish faces in simper, the same brown cows in ditches, the same white sails in squalls and the same slices of lemons in saucers." Art had become a fashion, style had degenerated into mannerism, and mannerism had fallen into pettiness.

The Pre-Raphaelites revolted against classicism as a foreign element introduced into England by Sir Joshua Reynolds and his contemporaries, for whom the later Italian schools represented all that is beautiful and desirable in art. They turned for aid and inspiration to mediaevalism, as to the rightful and common inheritance of the modern nations. They rejected the facility fatal to ideas, the artistic subterfuges and conventions of the followers of "the grand style;" seeking their guides and models in artists who lived in a time when human thought teemed, although it struggled with an imperfect medium of expression—sometimes even to the point of childishness. Thus in the old Italians and old Flemings they found their masters, whom they did not servilely imitate, but to whom they were attracted as to the founders of a national and popular art.

The mediaevalism of Rossetti, William Morris and Burne-Jones was real. It was due to natural impulse, fostered by judicious study, and revealed in sincere and beautiful forms, whether through the medium of pictorial, decorative, or poetic art, and whether derived from Italian, French, or Icelandic sources. In common with the men of the thirteenth and fourteenth centuries, the English Pre-Raphaelite poets and artists were restless, passionate and imaginative. Like them, too, they began their work imperfectly trained in technique. But all that was ingenuous and pardonable to the critic, in the early masters, became, in the modern Englishmen, open to the reproach of affectation, indolence and even degeneracy. Again, the subjects and titles chosen by the reformers and innovators were as new to the English ear, as were the forms and colors by which they expressed themselves in painting and decoration, strange to the English eye. These facts therefore became a lively cause for ridicule, which was further strengthened by a following gained for the Pre-Raphaelites among people of would-be refinement and little originality, to whom all that was singular in the new movement appealed, but who were, by nature, blind and deaf as to its true meaning and aims. So, as it is cleverly put in the opera of "Patience:" "My mediaevalism is not real," must have been the heart, if not the lip-confession of many a poseur of the eighteen seventies and eighties. At that time there were doubtless numerous replicas of Bunthorne, the "crushed" esthete, and of Archibald, who after his long wanderings in realms of faery and poesy, loyally returned to his milkmaid love.

A second declaration above quoted from "Patience," calls for special comment: "I love you with a fourteenth century Florentine frenzy." And as before intimated, this is no fortuitous alliterative combination of words. It is wit of the subtlest and keenest kind. It betrays a perfect appreciation of the thing caricatured, beside amusing the ear of the listener, just as the speaker of the sentence amuses his eye by a nameless touch of over "intensity," For the pictorial explanation of the phrase one has only to glance at certain of the pagan subjects of Botticelli, notably the famous "Spring"—

wherein the great decorative artist so admired by the English Pre-Raphaelites, has drawn together in a moving, dancing group the exuberant life, youth and strength typical of the Italian Revival of Letters.

In "Patience," Rossetti, William Morris and Burne-Jones receive each a share of lively good-natured pleasantry. Rossetti is a target for wit as the founder and master of the "Fleshly School of Poetry;" the reviver of obsolete forms of metre; the deviser of refrains in which sound overpowers sense, so that, as Bunthome is made to say of his own verses: "They mean nothing."

The parody upon William Morris appeals to the eye rather than to the ear. Bunthorne and the maidens are clothed in what may be called the transitional colors of the Morris firm of decorators. The pale olive garb of the Aesthete, the peacock blues and pomegranate tones seen in the robes of the chorus, were offered by Morris as the first protest of art against the aniline dyes of commerce, which he denounced as "hideous, crude, livid and cheap." Also, the sunflower, which is affected by Bunthorne and which grows dearer to him in proportion as he is "crushed," until in the last tableau he uses it as a solace and shield this too is a hidden recognition of the art-influence of Morris. He, as a decorator, criticised the double sunflower as "a coarse and dull plant," while he praised the single bloom of the same species as "both interesting and beautiful, with its sharply chiselled yellow florets relieved by the quaintly patterned sad-colored centre clogged with bees and butterflies." The preference of the artist, and his decorative use of a despised plant raised the single sunflower to such high favor that it spread from the British Isles to the aristocratic gardens of America, where it still blooms as a survival of the "Aesthetic Craze" of the early eighteen eighties.

But piquant and mirth-provoking as are the sarcasms in "Patience" against Rossetti and Morris, they yield in point of subtlety to those directed toward Burne-Jones. Every frequenter of picture-shops can recognize the originals of the "stained glass attitudes" of the funny dragoons, as they twist themselves into almost impossible contortions to gaze "soulfully" at their lilies. Nor are the gestures of the chorus less familiar, as the long, slender "devitalized" arms are extended in helpless adoration, or the sinuous bodies wave and writhe in an ecstasy of love and are each and all to be found in the Burne-Jones book of studies, and recur again and again in such masterpieces as the "Mirror of Venus," "Laus Veneris," "Le Chant d' Amour," and "Love Among the Ruins." Altogether, in view of the interest already noted and because of many subtleties untouched upon in the present slight criticism, the opera of "Patience" should be preserved as a "little classic," containing the rapidly drawn sketches of three most important figures in the art-life of the nineteenth century.

MORRIS AND BURNE-JONES.

ANY record of the life of William Morris would be indeed incomplete, unless it contained a more than passing reference to his faithful friend and sympathetic coadjutor, Edward Burne-Jones. The two were joined together by what would appear to be the strongest bond of human companionship: a community of tastes coupled with a diversity of temperament. To this union Morris furnished the masculine, and Burne-Jones the feminine element. The one was passionate often to the degree of violence, active, self-reliant, even aggressive. The other was contemplative, endowed with a Griselda-like patience, imaginative, idealistic. By blood both were Celts, strong in racial characteristics. In thought and art both were mediaevalists, with the distinction that Morris was attracted by Anglo-Norman architecture and literature; while the ideas and expression of Burne-Jones were colored with a pronounced Italianism. For this difference the first studies of each artist were partially responsible: the college library at Marlboro and the location of the college itself providing Morris with fine and abundant material for archeological research; while Burne-Jones is known to have received the impulse toward an artistic career from a drawing of Rossetti's, which fell into his hands during his freshman year at Oxford. In both men also the long course of years did but fulfil the initial impulse: Morris became a creator and inventor, bold, experimental, and epoch-making, like the builders of the thirteenth century, whom he acknowledged as his masters, models and guides; Burne-Jones, on the contrary, unique in genius and personality, labored in artistic solitude, caring little for the world's applause, and remaining faithful to his early ideals with a truly feminine constancy. The joint accomplishments of the two men produced upon the art of their time an influence that is quite immeasurable, as to depth, breadth and lasting effect. Together, they not only redeemed the English decorative arts from a decadent, denationalized state, but they carried them to a point which commanded acknowledgement and provoked imitation from France, Italy and Germany. Even in their separate, personal gifts in Morris poetical genius, in Burne-Jones pictorial power, they seemed to supplement, balance and support each other. They received mental impressions, the one from the other, with a rapidity and delicacy born of close companionship and the power to feel and see in common. But they advanced to this intellectual and spiritual sympathy from widely differing circumstances.

Unlike Morris, Burne-Jones contended in childhood and early youth with unfavorable surroundings. His innate faculties were tardily developed, and even when awakened, were matured only through invincible determination and patience. Three years the senior of his friend, he was born in Birmingham, in 1833, when as yet the name of this great factory-town, vulgarized into "Brummagem," stood for all that is commercially contemptible and spurious. He was the son of a small shopkeeper, and he grew up in an austere, dreary home, apart from the tender influence of woman, as his only sister, his elder by a few years, had died in her infancy, and his mother at his birth. Imaginative literature was forbidden him through the religious prejudices of his father, and the boy thus forced to a starvation whose pangs he but half realized, suffered on in silence and solitude, since he made but few acquaintances and opened his heart to none. Meanwhile his education was not neglected, as he was entered, at the age of eleven, at King Edward's School, by his father, who hoped to make him a clergyman of the Anglican Church. During the years of preparation for his destined profession, he acquired a knowledge and love of the classics and of history, which once he had met with his friend Morris, became the basis of extended readings and of wide general culture.

At twenty, Burne-Jones passed into Exeter College, Oxford, meeting Morris on the first day of term, within a week becoming his inseparable friend, and afterward writing of him:

"From the first I knew how different he was from all the men I had ever met. He talked with vehemence, and sometimes with violence. I never knew him languid or tired."

This first appreciation continued to be the same in kind and degree. For whenever BurneJones wrote or spoke of his friend, it was with a half-feminine admiration for the aggressive, sturdy, path-making qualities in which he himself was altogether lacking. The undivided intimacy of the two undergraduates continued throughout their residence at Oxford, each giving and taking his share in all that made for intellectual advancement, the widening of interests and the opening of new vistas of thought and life. Burne-Jones, filled with enthusiasm for the Celtic and Scandinavian mythologies, gave the impulse which led to the greatest literary achievement of Morris. His companionship, too, did much to raise art to a place by the side of literature in the daily life of his friend, since his characteristic drawings, known as "Jones's Devils," and sought after by his fellow-students, aroused the latent manual dexterity of Morris, who shortly began to cover the margins of his books and letters with architectural *motifs* and floriated ornament.

The close bond between the two young men extended until it included four or five others filled with the same aspirations toward beauty and the same indefinite desires to do something for humanity; each wishing to act according to his own will and way. Thus three years passed, during which Morris developed into the most original young poet of England. At the end of this period, Burne-Jones, sensitive and susceptible, yielded to the virile personality of Rossetti, and sank completely under his influence. Through the advice of the Pre-Raphaelite leader, the novice enthusiast began at once to paint, without academic training, or the craftsmanship necessary to an artist. Rossetti maintained that the enforced drudgery of copying from the antique would blunt, if it did not destroy, the delicate imagination of his younger friend: an opinion taken not without reason, but which strictly carried out as it was, might have led to disaster, had the strenuous later efforts of Burne-Jones not atoned for the deficiencies of his first work. Indeed, as he once remarked of himself, in the technique of his art, at twenty-five he was but fifteen, and before he could adequately express the depth of his feeling and the beauty of his conceptions, he was forced to submit himself to the ordeal of patient toil. Two years of study under the direction of Rossetti constituted his sole art-education, if we except the fertile production, the constant observation and experiment which finally rendered him the greatest self-made painter of modern times. At fifty, he had become a subtle, exquisite draughtsman, a consummate master of color, an artist of so pronounced a personality as to be recognized in the slightest sketch coming from his hand. His faults, his exaggerations, like those of Botticelli, to whom he offers many points of resemblance, seemed to proceed not from ignorance, or lack of perception, but rather from fixed principles inherent in his qualities as a great decorative painter. In some scheme known to himself alone lay, without doubt, the explanation of his peculiar treatment of the human body: the small head, the great height and slenderness, the weight thrown upon one foot, the inward arch of the stiffened leg, the contrast in curve between the supporting and the supported side, and the other points noted without explanation by the French critic, M. de la Sizeranne, who seems not to recall that precisely the same treatment prevailed among the later sculptors of Greece: a fact which, in view of the intense studiousness of Burne-Jones, indicates that the artist followed a definite system, instead of repeating technical errors, until his senses were so perverted that he saw beauty where only ugliness existed. Another indication of an underlying system in the work of Burne-Jones is found in his *selectiveness*. His book of "studies," or preliminary drawings, shows how carefully his first intentions were modified again and again, in order that they might fit together and become integral parts of an important picture. His was certainly a completeness laboriously acquired. He attained an expressive line, but it was not through economic draughtsmanship. He had no affinity with artists like Flaxman, Durer, Hokosai, the eighteenth century Japanese, or Forain, the modern Frenchman, in whose sketches—spontaneous and yet restrained—it would be difficult to say where each line stops and where each begins.

Consequent upon this selectiveness: that is the power to choose, absorb and assimilate, Burne-Jones offered frequently in his work suggestions of earlier artists whom he had closely, but never servilely, studied. He was no borrower or thief, but simply an honest, legitimate inheritor of the great capital and patrimony of art. His most marked preference was, of course, for Botticelli, with whom he saw and felt in common. Titian taught him much in the handling of the orchestra of color. Michelangelo's "Slaves" writhe on the English painter's "Wheel of Fortune," as they were purposed to suffer on the tomb of Pope Julius Second. Leonardo often opened to him the secret of his alluring curves. But it is simple justice to assert that, strengthened and formed by his contact with Italian and Greek art, Burne-Jones never falsified his distinctive personality. He recognized his own wherever he found it, mastered it and then displayed it without fear of question or criticism.

These unvarying methods, adopted early in life and pursued throughout an art-career of forty years, the gradual gathering of materials, the slow evolution of a picture which sometimes extended through a decade or more, offer extreme contrasts with the ways of Morris, the closely allied brother-in-art of Burne-Jones. For the first named, a few months or weeks sufficed for gaining the theory and practice of any subject to which he applied himself. He labored with a "furia" worthy of Michelangelo. He produced in great quantity and at rapid rate. His devotion, absolute for the time being, was given successively to a number of interests, widely differing among themselves. He loved, accepted the gift which the thing loved had to bestow. and passed on to new conquests. He was in all things the complement and opposite of his friend, who lived apart from men and their concerns, cloistered in his art, devoutly attendant upon the Revelation of Beauty.

And thus, but for William Morris, the influence of Burne-Jones might ever have remained confined to aristocratic circles; since the possession of great examples of pictorial art is the privilege of the few and wealthy. Owing to the labors of the skilled artisan and apostle of democracy, the barriers of individual ownership were cast down, and the work of his richly endowed friend was scattered broadcast among the people through the medium of decorative design. It has been said that "it would be a serious undertaking to measure the flood of beauty poured by the two co-laborers into the world." But an idea of the greatness of their accomplishment may be formed from the statement of a trustworthy critic, who declares simply and without the emphasis that fears contradiction, that "they reformed the taste of England." The churches, the colleges, the municipal museums and the homes of their own country bear witness to their genius which, exercised as if sent forth from a single brain, glorified and transfigured everything that it touched; so that the arts and crafts of the Middle Ages rose again, and the workshop was restored to the high place which it occupied in the times when Florence and Nuremberg and the cathedral cities of France teemed with simple, sturdy burghers, whose first care was to preserve, through common effort and organization, the traditions of their skill, and whose lives were consecrated to the religion of beauty.

Consequent upon the decorative reform in England, the Applied Arts have risen from their decadence in France and have become firmly established in the United States among a people most ready of all to receive the lessons of a true aestheticism. And thus the chance meeting of two youths, a half-century since, on the benches of an Oxford College, led to the opening of a vista into the past, wherein we see the ancestors of the modern nations building and carving, painting and spinning, throwing into their work their strength, their love and very souls. And the lesson to be learned from the vision is that a real art, created by the people for the people, is able not only to beautify, but also to simplify life, to unify the interests of all sorts and conditions of men, and finally to realize the meaning of the word *commonwealth*.

WILLIAM MORRIS

When the change comes, it will embrace the whole of society, and there will be no discontented ckss left to form the elements of a fresh revolution. It is necessary that the movement should not be ignorant, but intelligent. What I should like to have now far more than anything else, would be a body of able, highminded, competent men, who should act as instructors. I should look to those men to preach what Socialism really is not a change for the sake of change, but a change involving the very noblest ideal of human life and duty: a life in which every human being should find unrestricted scope for his best powers and faculties.

WILLIAM MORRIS:
First public utterance, after becoming member of Socialistic League.

Education is the prime necessity, and it is hopeless to attempt to reconstruct society without the existing materials.

WILLIAM MORRIS:
Letter to Lady Burne-Jones, September, 1883.

I could never forget that in spite of all drawbacks, my work is little less than pleasure to me; that under no conceivable circumstances would I give it up, even if I could. Over and over again, I have asked myself why should not my lot be the common lot. My work is simple work enough; much of it, nor that the least pleasant, any man of decent intelligence could do, if he could but get to care about the work and its results. Indeed, I have been ashamed when I have thought of the contrast between my happy working hours and the unpraised, unrewarded, monotonous drudgery which most men are condemned to. Nothing shall convince me that such labour as this is good or necessary to civilization.

WILLIAM MORRIS:
Lecture: "Art, Wealth & Riches" -Manchester Royal Institution, March 6, 1883.

AN ARGUMENT FOR SIMPLICITY IN HOUSEHOLD FURNISHINGS

IN all that concerns household furnishings and decoration, present . tendencies are toward a simplicity unknown in the past. The form of any object is made to express the structural idea directly, frankly, often almost with baldness. The materials employed are chosen no longer solely for their intrinsic value, but with a great consideration for their potential beauty. The qualities thus apprehended are traced to their source and then carefully developed by the skill of the craftsman.

In the eighteenth century, the French cabinet makers created charming objects suited to the palaces and castles of the old nobility. They revelled in richness of material: in woods brought from countries and colonies difficult of access; in costly gilding and other applied ornament; in fanciful painting which exquisite delicacy of handling alone saved from triviality and insignificance.

But today, with the idea of development everywhere dominant, in the sciences, in educational methods, in all that furthers human intercourse, comfort and progress we find the mood of the century impressed upon the material and necessary objects by which we are surrounded. Even our beds, tables and chairs, if planned and executed according to the newer and sounder ideas of household art, offer us a lesson taught by their form, substance and finish. We are no longer tortured by exaggerated lines the reasons for which are past divining. We have not to deal with falsifying veneers, or with disfiguring so-called ornament. We are not necessarily confronted by substances precious because of their traditional use, their rarity, and the difficulty attending their attainment. We are, first of all, met by plain shapes which not only declare, but emphasize their purpose. Our eyes rest on materials which, gathered from the forests, along the streams, and from other sources familiar to us, are, for that reason, interesting and eloquent. We may, in the arms of our reading-chair, or in the desk before which we pass our working-day, study the striking undulations in the grain of oak, ash, elm, or other of our native woods, and in so doing, learn the worth of patient, well-directed and skilled labor; of that labor which educates; that is: leads out and develops the hidden Values and qualities of things too often neglected because they are frequently seen.

PRO PATRIA

WHEN in the decade of 1870-1880, Oriental art began to receive wide-spread attention in France, and became a favorite topic of conversation in fashionable salons, there were many connoisseurs who denied its claims to consideration. Then it was that M. Thiers, the President of the French Republic, summed up in a single pithy sentence the reasons for the narrow prejudice which refused currency to ideas other than those consecrated by long familiarity.

He declared: "One should not go to Japan with the Parthenon in one's mind."

A similar prejudice has established itself in this country regarding the use of mahogany in the finer pieces of household furnishings. The preference for this wood, founded partially upon its beauty, received a very strong impetus from the connection of the wood and of certain famous cabinet makers with our colonial history, which of late has been so thoroughly treated by American authors, and so thoroughly studied by our patriotic clubs. Consequently, our native products have been neglected and their possibilities overlooked. But it is true that oak, ash and elm, properly treated, possess attractions that yield to those of no other woods. The undulations of their grain, the soft, unobtrusive tones which they assume through skillful polish, the color-play which runs over their smooth surface are qualities which to be appreciated need only to be fairly observed. The intelligent craftsman in our country is now raising our northern woods to a. place beside that occupied by the long-admired mahogany.

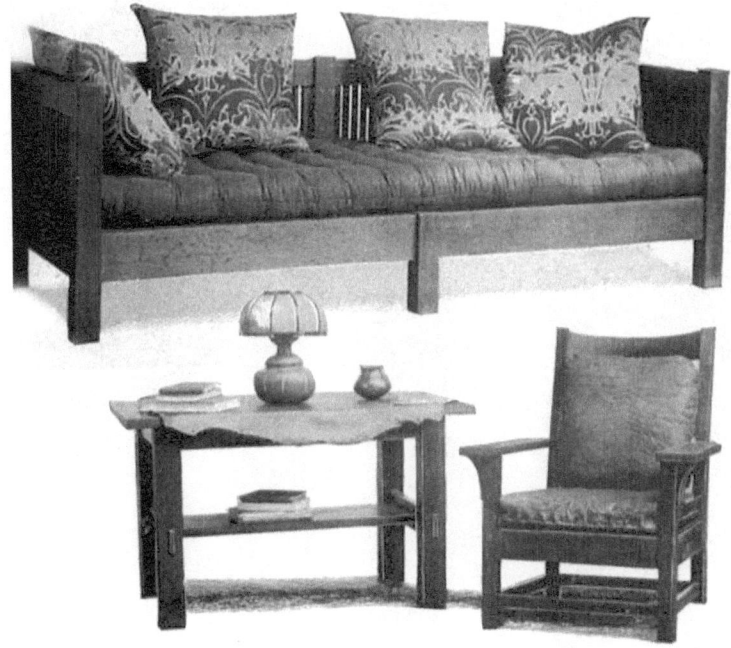

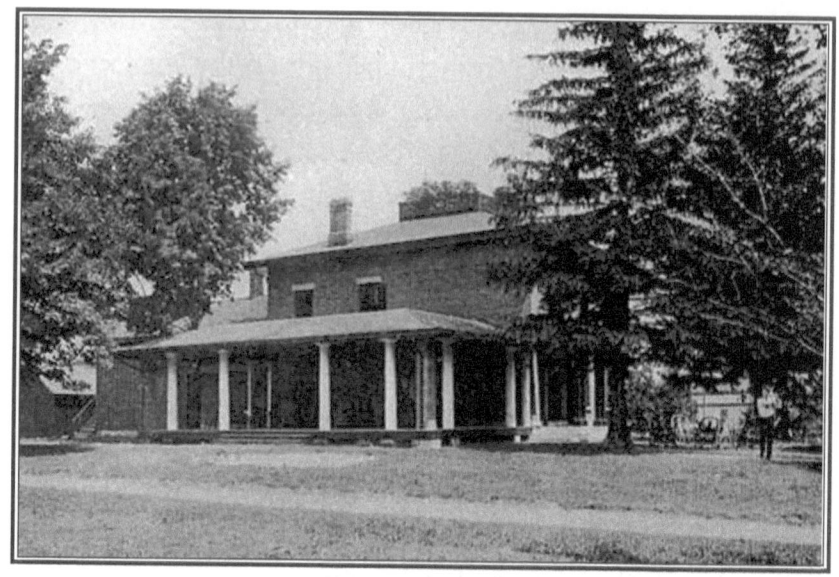

Onondaga Golf Club, Syracuse, NY

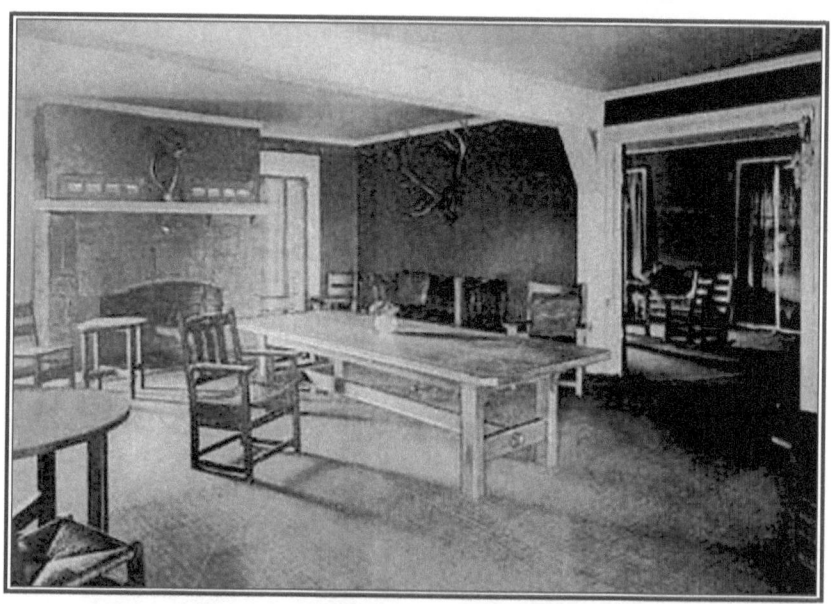

Interior view of Golf Club

THE CRAFTSMAN

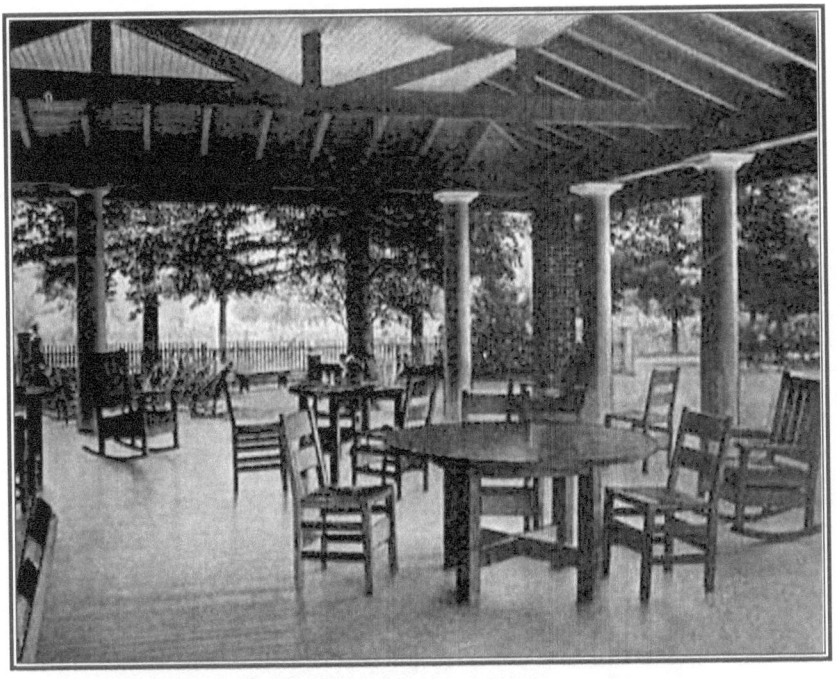

View of Veranda - Onondaga Golf Club, Syracuse, NY

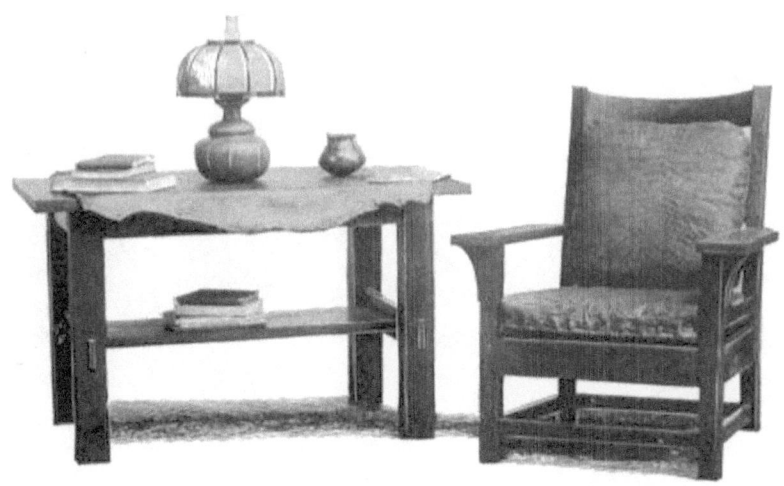

THE CRAFTSMAN

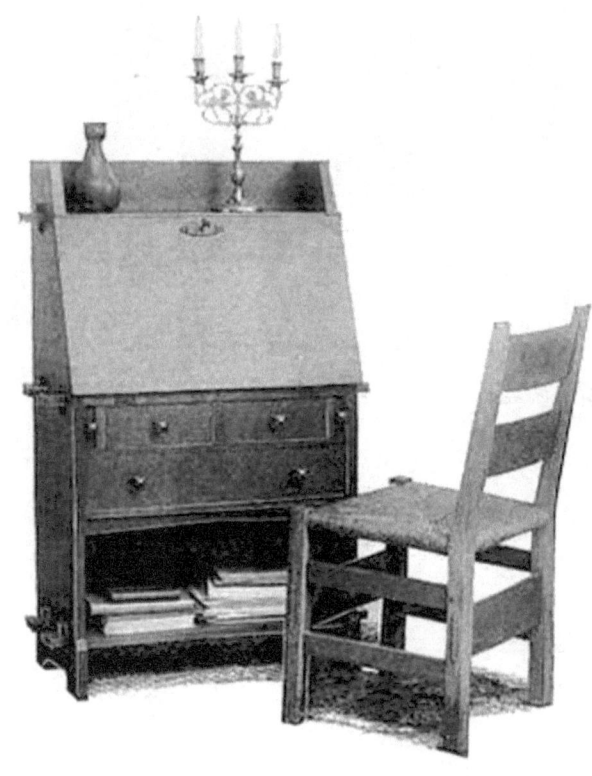

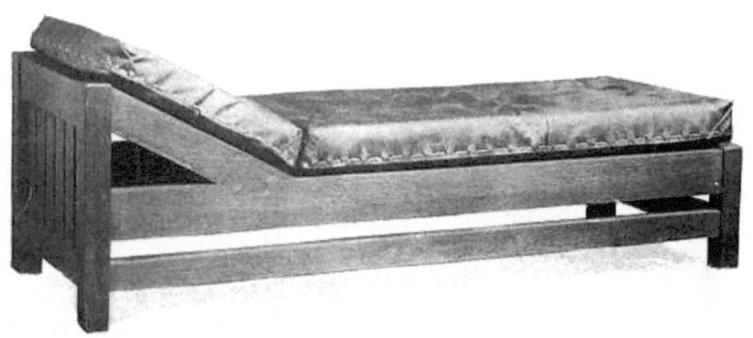

THE CRAFTSMAN

STYLE AND ITS REQUISITES

THE most exquisite things in nature and in art are those which possess an indefinable quality called style. The piece of literature, the architectural work, the beautiful woman, the flower wanting in this last nameless grace are alike unfortunate. For in order to gain recognition and appreciation in a highly civilized age, distinction, that is to say: separation from one's kind is necessary. But this distinction must be natural and inherent: never sought after, assumed, or forced. In the case of objects created by the artist, style must be a part of the very conception; and not something consciously added in the mechanical execution.

The masters of style, the chiefs of the great schools wrought in obedience to impulse, because they were forced from within; because the thing seen in their mental vision cried out to be born, to become materialized. The lintel, the column, the arch were not incorporated into the building art by deliberate selection, by critics and learned experimentalists. The structural element was seized by the master and fell into place beneath his powerful grasp: the result representing what we recognize now as Greek, or Roman, or mediaeval. Nor did the two great Italians, Raphael and Michelangelo, stride after their distinguishing traits. The harmonic composition of the one, the infinite linear variety of the other were spontaneous, constant forces which needed not to be fed or fostered by their possessors, of which they were a vital part; living with them, and passing away at the death of the masters, never again to be repeated.

Style is therefore the quality and rightful possession of one individual, or class of individuals. Outside of these limits, it is a false and unjustifiable assumption. We feel this statement to be true when we pause to analyse the impressions that often fall like discords upon our senses, as we go upon our ways of work or pleasure. For example, the sixteenth century French castle architecture is "sui generis." It is incomparable in its way. It lends itself to the nature in the midst of which it was created; rising from the landscape of the river Loire as a sympathetic response to the appeal of the sky, the water, the hills and the forests. Further than this, it represents the time of its birth. Its splendor of material, its brilliancy of execution, its imaginative, luxuriant, graceful ornament recall the artistic, pleasure-loving Francis First who passed with his court from chateau to chateau; avoiding his burgher-capital, Paris, lest his waste of health should incite the honest artisans and shopkeepers to discontent and insurrection.

Now, let a reproduction of this style be attempted in the heart of our American metropolis, as has been done in several notable instances. The result is no longer either pleasing to the student and connoisseur, or satisfying to the masses. The feudal architecture is by centuries out of place in a modern city, presumably the home of civic law and order. The broad avenues, teeming with the life, movement and inventions of a scientific age, form an incongruous setting for these old-time jewels of art. The fantastic ornament, the gargoyles and griffons which over-run the whole and cut the sky-line in a hundred curious ways have no longer a reason for existence. They have lost the sense of mystery with which they were once invested. Their meaning has passed from the vital state into the domain of historical interest. In the evolution of art, their place has long been supplanted.

We can thus go on selecting examples at will, and sure always of arriving at the same conclusion. As we pass through the Place Vendome, Paris, we are at once impressed by the formal, stately grandeur of the surrounding architecture. The eager shopper with his eyes still dazzled by the glittering frivolities of the rue de la Paix is unconsciously sobered by confronting the grave buildings of the historic square; while the student delights to imagine the space as it must have appeared under Louis le Grand: animated by lumbering coaches and gilded sedan-chairs, with their freight of pompous gentlemen in flowing wigs, and of ladies in heavy velvet and brocade gowns.

Again, as in the first case cited, let the externals of this style be copied in America. The result will be a spiritless, literal translation, wanting the life and soul of the original. A sense of unfitness and unreality will forever pervade and haunt the imitation which through the lack of spontaneity, has no justification for being; which has no basis of artistic truth, and which represents no dominant thought of the period.

So, advancing from instance to instance, foe reach the conclusion that any art worthy of the name must strike its roots deep into the life of the people, and must produce as freely and naturally as does the plant in summer. We have thus far drawn our examples from architecture, but as the smaller is contained in the greater, so are the lesser arts related to that of the builder. Sculpture and painting are its handmaids, and household decoration its adjunct and ally.

The objects which form our material environment exert upon us an influence that is not to be withstood. If we, our children and

THE CRAFTSMAN

our successors are to be true citizens and integral parts of the Commonwealth, we must choose carefully the objects by which .toe surround ourselves; bringing our judgment to bear upon them as fully as we do upon our books, our studies and our companions. We must support an art created by the people for the people: simple, sincere and structural; an art wherein the designer and the craftsman shall be one and the same individual, creating for his own pleasure and unassailed by commercialism.

It is in this spirit that the Master and Associates of the United Crafts produce their work and await results.

The artistic quality of the Rush or Reed has been generally ignored by the cabinet-maker. We strength and durability of its fibre have largely caused its employment. But it lends itself easily to aesthetic color and textile schemes. Made soft and pliable, and retaining its natural variegations, it gives a whole gamut of greens, 'with occasional rusty glints punctuating what otherwise were a too spiritless mass of color. It is then often combined with the mellow tones of" "fumed oak" as we find it in certain chairs and seats recently produced in the workshops of the United Crafts. The combination cannot be otherwise than a perfect one, as it is based upon Nature as displayed in the autumn woods.

The examples of cabinet-making shown in this book are from the workshops of the United Crafts, Eastwood, NY.

THE CRAFTSMAN

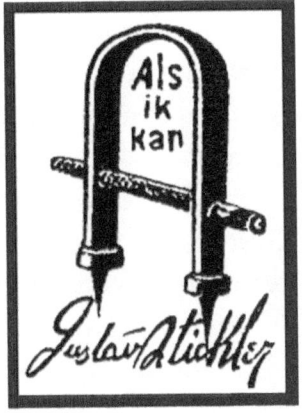

In the Middle Ages, that golden period of the arts and crafts, each master-workman adopted some device or legend which, displayed upon every object of his creation, came finally to represent his individuality as completely as did his face, or his voice; making him known beyond the burgher circle in which he passed his life, and, after his death, becoming a magic formula, by which to conjure up his memory, even though the years had multiplied into centuries.

Among the legends so employed, the one assumed by Jan van Eyck, the early Flemish painter, has retained its force and power down to our own day. *Als ich kanne* (if I can) appears written across the canvases of this fourteenth century *chef d'ecole,* placed there, without doubt, as an inspiration toward excellence in that art wherein van Eyck became an epoch maker. Appearing in the background of nis masterful portraits, it has something of defiance and humor, as if offering a covert challenge to those less skillful. The *Als ich kanne* of van Eyck, like the *Quand mer* of Sarah Bernhardt, reflects that sentiment of courage, boldness and persistency which appeals to all truly virile natures. Thus when William Morris, in his early manhood, visited the Low Countries and there grew fired with enthusiasm for the decorative arts, he found this legend and made it his own. He used it, in French translation, first in tapestries designed for his own dwelling, and finally it became identified with him; so that the *Si je puis* not only recalls his memory as vividly as do the designs which speak to us from the hangings of our walls, the tiles of our floors, or the cover of the books which lie upon our tables.

The same legend in its modern Flemish form, *Als ik kanne* has been adopted by the Master of the United Crafts. It here forms an interesting device with a joiner's compass, which is the most primitive and distinctive tool of the worker in wood. This legend is further accompanied by the signature of the Master of the Crafts, Gustave Stickley, which, together with the proper date, appears branded upon every object produced in the workshop of the Guild. In this way, authenticity is assured, comparisons of progress are made possible, and every facility of information is afforded the one who shall acquire the piece.

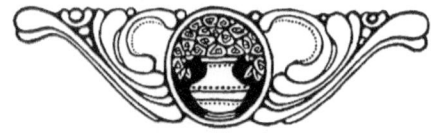

PRODUCTION NOTES

Chapter Headings and some headlines have been printed in 14pt. True Golden.

Body Text in 11 pt. Galliard

ADDITIONAL RESOURCES

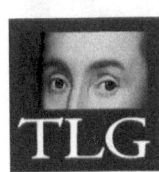

The Long Gallery
thelonggallery.blogspot.com
twitter: @thelonggallery

Website featuring news, opinion, resources & features on Medieval, Tudor & 19th-20th Century Revival Architecture, Style, Art & Design.

The ArchRevivalist Daily
paper.li/thelonggallery/archrevivalist

Our daily News updates covering Heritage and Preservation News, Medieval and Renaissance history, culture art and design, traditional building methods and related subjects.

THE LONG GALLERY

Visit
The Long Gallery

A great sources for news, opinion, resources & features about Medieval, Tudor & 19th-20th Century Revival Architecture, Style, Art & Design. Book reviews, DIY stories, tips and more!

thelonggallery.blogspot.com

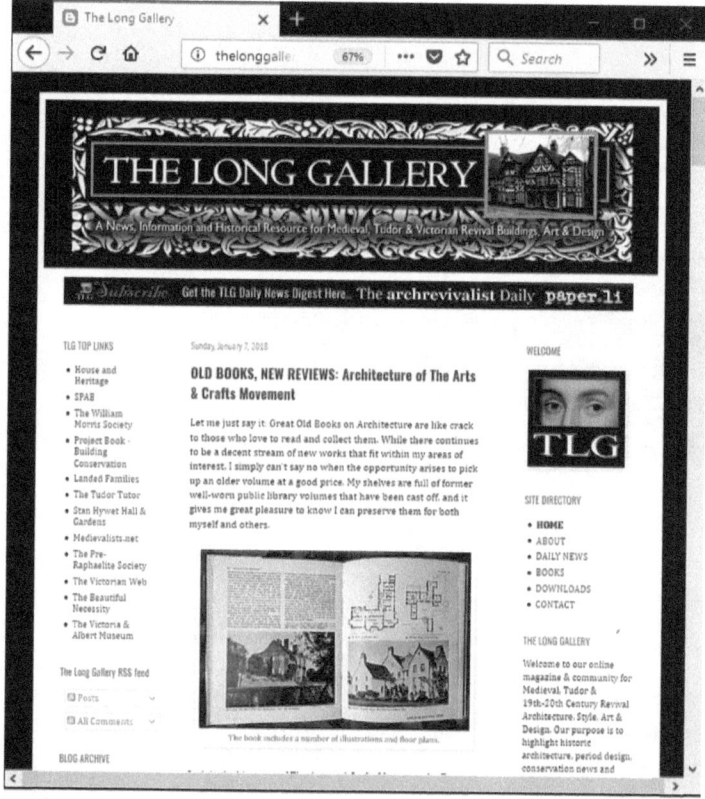

THE LONG GALLERY

NOTES

www.ingramcontent.com/pod-product-compliance
Lightning Source LLC
Chambersburg PA
CBHW031536210526
45464CB00003B/1034